Bible Heroes: Abraham, Joseph, and Moses

by Dee Leone

illustrated by Janet Armbrust

Cover by Bron Smith
Copyright © 1994, Shining Star Publications
ISBN No. 0-382-30480-2
Standardized Subject Code TA ac
Printing No. 98765432

Shining Star Publications
1204 Buchanan St., Box 299
Carthage, IL 62321-0299

The purchase of this book entitles the buyer to reproduce student activity pages for classroom use only. Any other use requires written permission from Shining Star Publications.

All rights reserved. Printed in the United States of America.

Unless otherwise indicated, the New International Version of the Bible was used in preparing the activities of this book.

Dedication

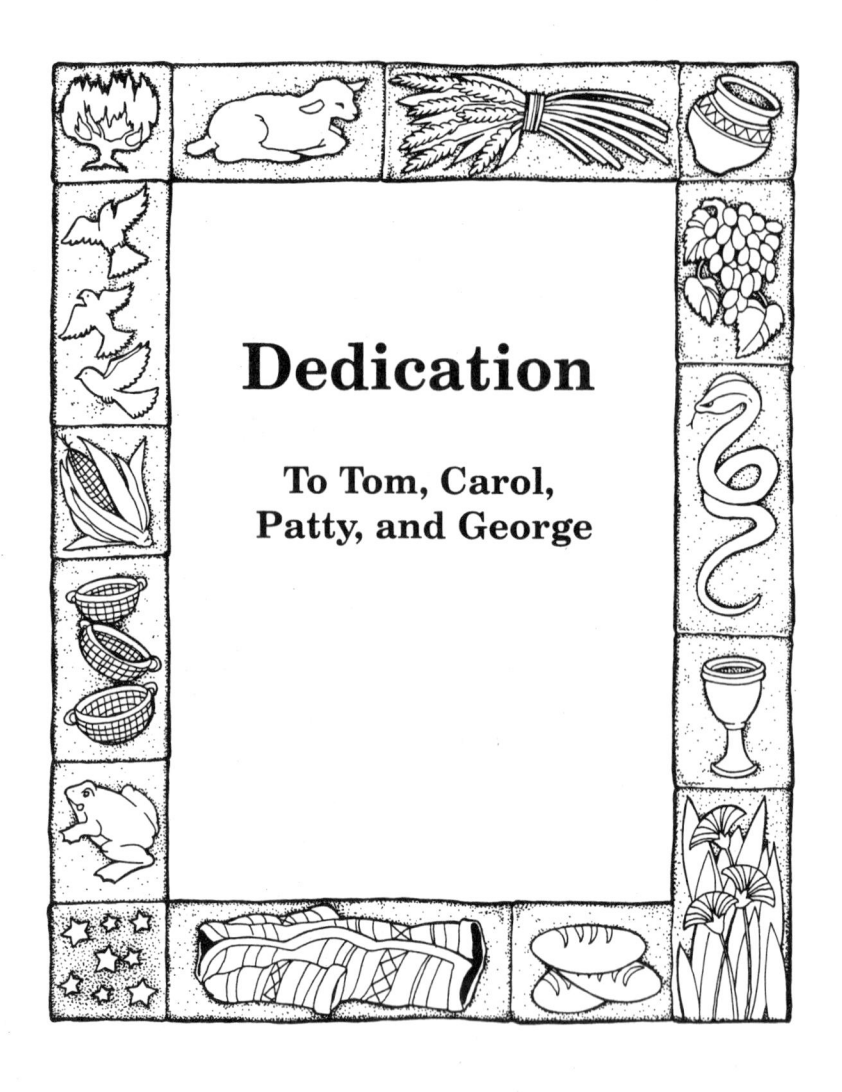

To Tom, Carol,
Patty, and George

To the Teacher/Parent

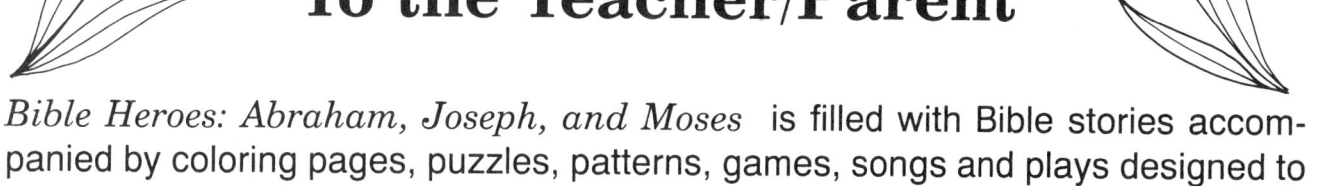

Bible Heroes: Abraham, Joseph, and Moses is filled with Bible stories accompanied by coloring pages, puzzles, patterns, games, songs and plays designed to make each child's study of these three Bible characters real celebrations!

Each unit begins with a Bible story to introduce your children to the Bible hero. This is followed by a page of activity suggestions and patterns. The reproducible coloring book pages reinforce story concepts and help children visualize Bible scenes.

Each coloring book page has a corresponding activity page. For example, "God Speaks to Abram," the first coloring page, goes with "God Calls Abram," the first activity page. You may want to have the children complete a coloring page and the corresponding activity page on the same day. After all the coloring pages of a unit have been discussed and completed, they may be made into keepsake story booklets.

The patterns included in each unit may be used to create puppets and other visual aids to make the story, songs, and plays come alive. Patterns may be backed with felt for use on a flannelboard, or they may be attached to ice-cream sticks to create puppets for use with a box stage. Enlarged patterns may be made into paper bag puppets or stick masks, or used to create bulletin boards, mobiles, murals, props, and backdrops.

The songs in this book may be used to turn the plays into musicals. The words are sung to familiar tunes. In addition, games and crafts are included to reinforce Bible story concepts.

A number of exciting activities may be used to end each unit. For example, children may display their crafts on a table and invite others to their Bible hero "museum." Another fun way to end the units would be to play the games and use related objects as prizes. These might include toy frogs for the Moses games or star stickers for the Abraham game. Pencil toppers made from the Bible patterns in this book also make good prizes. Of course, one of the best ways to culminate each unit would be with a performance of the plays and songs – a sure way to delight audiences of all ages!

Table of Contents

Abraham

The Story of Abraham 5
Celebrating Abraham 6
Bible Story Coloring Pages 7-9
Activity Puzzles 10-15
Abraham/Moses Mask 16
Patterns, Props, and Plays 17-19
Songs 20
Game: Abraham's Picture Game 21-22
Arts and Crafts: Abraham Art 23

Joseph

The Story of Joseph 24
Celebrating Joseph 25
Bible Story Coloring Pages 26-28
Activity Puzzles 29-34
Pharaoh Mask 35
Patterns, Props, and Plays 36-38
Songs 39
Game: Saving for the Famine 40-41
Arts and Crafts: An Ornamented Coat 42

Moses

The Story of Moses 43
Celebrating Moses 44
Bible Story Coloring Pages 45-47
Activity Puzzles 48-53
Princess Mask 54
Puppet Patterns, Props, and Plays 55-57
Songs 58
Games: Pharaoh Fun and Moses Memory Match 59-60
Arts and Crafts: Moses Masterpieces 61
Answer Key 62

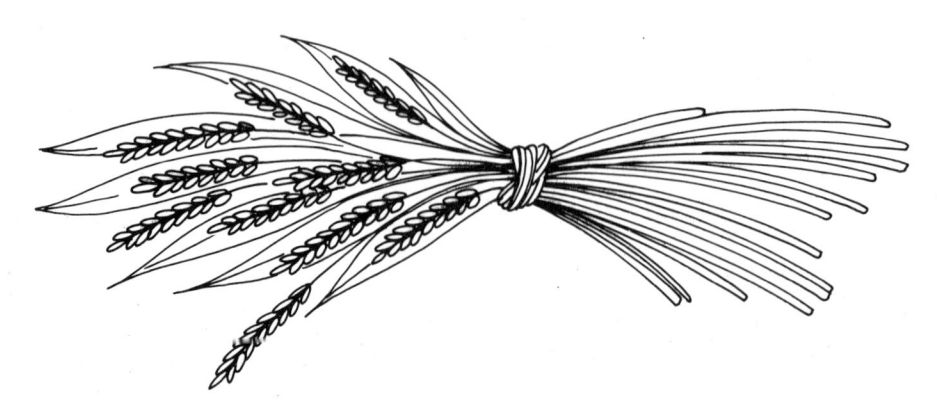

The Story of Abraham

Based on Genesis 12–13; 15; 17:1-8, 15-22; 18:1-15; 21:1-7; 24

(Note: Use the patterns on page 17 to create flannelboard pieces, stick puppets, or play props to emphasize the underlined words in the story.)

One day God told Abram to leave his country and go to another land. Abram took his wife, Sarai, and his relative, Lot, and set out. When he reached the great tree of Moreh at Shechem, the Lord appeared to him and said that the land would one day belong to Abram's offspring. Abram built an altar there to the Lord, then moved on. He pitched his tent and built another altar to the Lord. When there was famine in the land, Abram went to Egypt where he acquired many sheep, cattle, donkeys, camels, and servants.

When Abram left Egypt he was very rich. Lot, who left Egypt with him, also had lots of animals. In fact, the two had so many possessions the land could not support them all. There were many quarrels between their herdsmen. Abram said to Lot, "Let's not have any more fighting. Let's separate. You choose the land to the left or right. I will go in the opposite direction."

Lot took his animals and set off in one direction. Abram moved his tent and went to live near the great trees of Mamre. There the Lord spoke to Abram again. He said, "Look up at the sky and count the stars, if you can, for your descendents will be as numerous as the stars."

Abram was ninety-nine years old when the Lord appeared to him the next time. "You will no longer be called Abram," said the Lord. "You will be called Abraham, for I will make you the father of many nations. Your wife will no longer be called Sarai. She will be called Sarah, because she will have a son and will be the mother of nations." Abraham wondered how all this could happen, for he and his wife were so old. But God said that it would indeed happen.

One hot day as Abraham was sitting at the entrance to his tent, he looked up and saw three visitors. He bowed before them saying, "Do not pass me by. Let water be brought for washing your feet and food be brought for you to eat." Then he hurried into the tent and told Sarah to bake some bread. Next, he got a calf for a servant to prepare. When all was ready, he set the food before the visitors. Then the Lord told Abraham that his wife would have a son the next year. Sarah heard and laughed from inside the tent, for she thought she was too old to have a child. But sure enough, Sarah gave birth to a baby boy the next year and named him Isaac. Sarah said, "God has brought me laughter, and everyone who hears that I gave Abraham a son in his old age will laugh with me."

When Isaac grew up, Abraham sent a servant back to the land of his relatives to find Isaac a wife. The servant took some of Abraham's camels and set off. When he got to the town of Nahor, he had the camels kneel by the well outside town. It was time for the women of the town to come out to draw water. The servant prayed to the Lord, "When I ask for a drink and one of the daughters of the townspeople says, 'Drink, and I'll water your camels too,' let her be the one You have chosen to be Isaac's wife." Soon a beautiful girl named Rebekah came to get water. When the servant asked for water, she gave him a drink and said she would water his camels too. The servant knew Rebekah had been chosen to be Isaac's wife, and he took her with him. Isaac married Rebekah and they had children. Abraham's descendents became too numerous to count, like the stars in the sky.

Celebrating Abraham

Abraham's All-Star Activities

1. Write Bible verses such as Genesis 15:5 on the stars for children to memorize. Display them on a bulletin board entitled "Reach for the Stars." Each time a child memorizes a verse, add a star sticker to his certificate.

2. Have children read Bible stories about Abraham. Children can fill out stars with their names and the titles of the books they read. Then they can add the stars to a bulletin board. Use the Abraham certificate as a reading award.

3. Use the stars as name tags for a post-play reception at which star-shaped cookies are served. Near each plate of cookies, place stars on which verses from the story of Abraham are written.

4. Use the star as a pencil topper for a job well-done, or add it to the top of a heavy strip of paper to create a Bible bookmark.

5. Use the certificate as an invitation to a play or an Abraham art show, as an award for a star performance or completion of the Abraham coloring booklet, as a take-home memory verse card, or as a thank-you note.

Abram and Lot

God blessed Abram, and he became rich in livestock. The land could not support all his animals and Lot's too, so the two agreed to separate. Abram let Lot choose the land he wanted first.

2

God Speaks to Abram

God told Abram to leave his country and go to another land. So Abram gathered his people and his possessions and set out as God had told him.

Three Visitors

One day, when Abraham was sitting at the entrance to his tent, Abraham had three visitors. He had a meal prepared for them. Then the Lord said Abraham and Sarah would have a son the next year.

4

The Father of Many

God told Abraham that his descendents would be as numerous as the stars. He gave Abram a new name, Abraham, which means "father of many."

3

Shining Star Publications, Copyright © 1994

SS3840

Abraham's Request

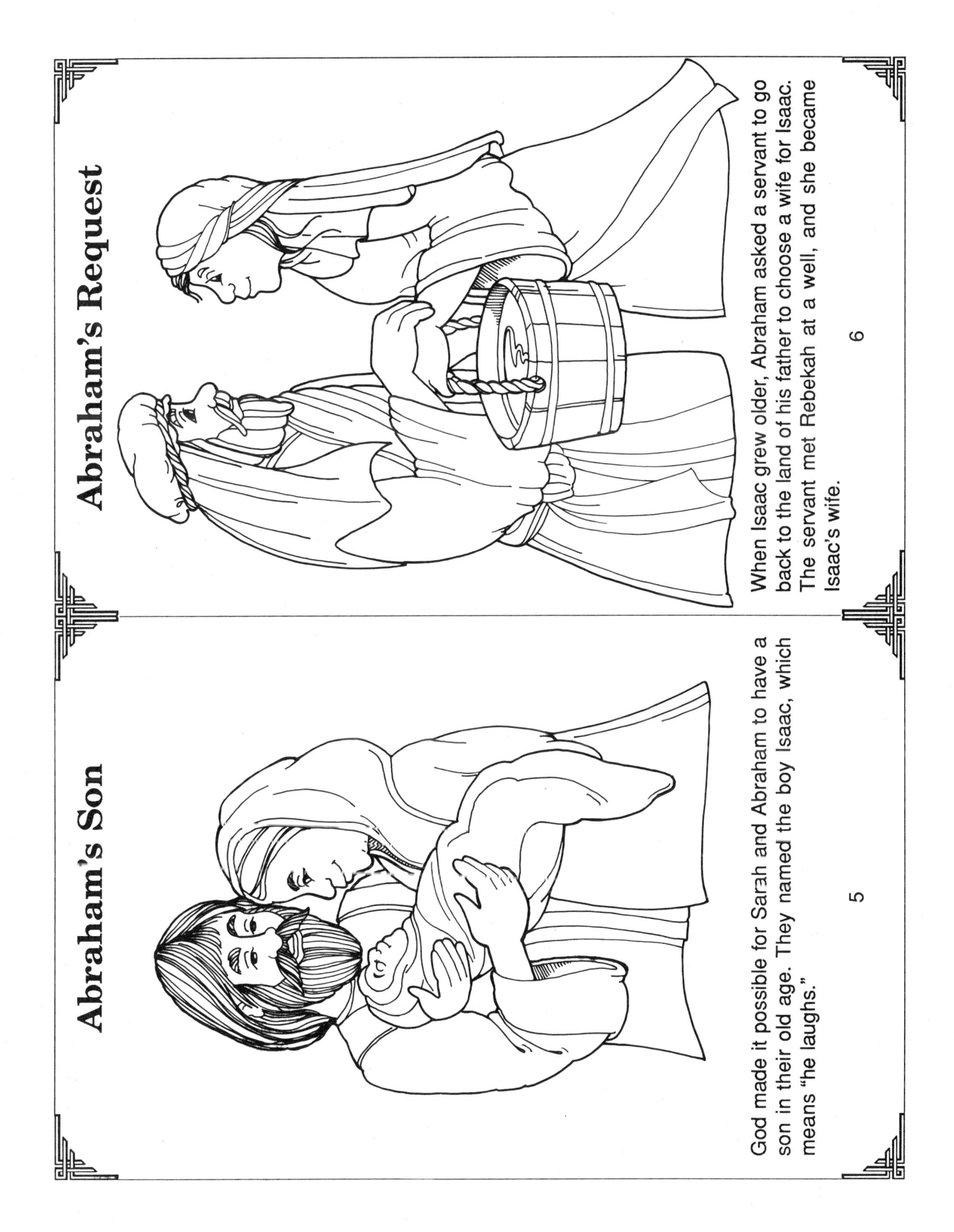

When Isaac grew older, Abraham asked a servant to go back to the land of his father to choose a wife for Isaac. The servant met Rebekah at a well, and she became Isaac's wife.

6

Abraham's Son

God made it possible for Sarah and Abraham to have a son in their old age. They named the boy Isaac, which means "he laughs."

5

God Calls Abraham

Write the letters with a 1 above them in order on the first blank. Write those with a 2 in order on the second blank. Do this for all eighteen words.

5	1	8	13	9	3	14	2	7	12	4	8	17	3	9
P	L	F	T	H	C	L	Y	Y	T	Y	A	S	O	O
17	6	11	8	1	14	3	10	7	16	2	18	8	16	3
H	A	G	T	E	A	U	A	O	W	O	Y	H	I	N
5	16	1	9	10	6	18	11	3	15	7	9	5	8	13
E	L	A	U	N	N	O	O	T	I	U	S	O	E	H
17	2	9	14	4	9	1	8	14	3	9	13	4	5	18
O	U	E	N	O	H	V	R	D	R	O	E	U	P	U
7	16	4	9	3	17	5	8	1	12	2	6	9	5	10
R	L	R	L	Y	W	L	S	E	O	R	D	D	E	D

"The Lord had said to Abram,

'_____ _____ _____,
    1   2   3

_____ _____
    4   5

_____ _____ _____,
    6   7   8

_____ _____
    9   10

_____ _____ _____ _____ _____
   11   12   13   14   15

_____ _____ _____.' "
   16   17   18

Genesis 12:1

Abram and Lot's Riches

Abram became very wealthy in silver and gold, as well as in camels, donkeys, cattle, and sheep. Lot did also. Circle ten possessions in the bottom picture that are not in the top picture.

"But the land could not support them while they stayed together, for their possessions were so great that they were not able to stay together." Genesis 13:6

The Stars in the Sky

Complete the verse by filling in the matching letter on each numbered line.

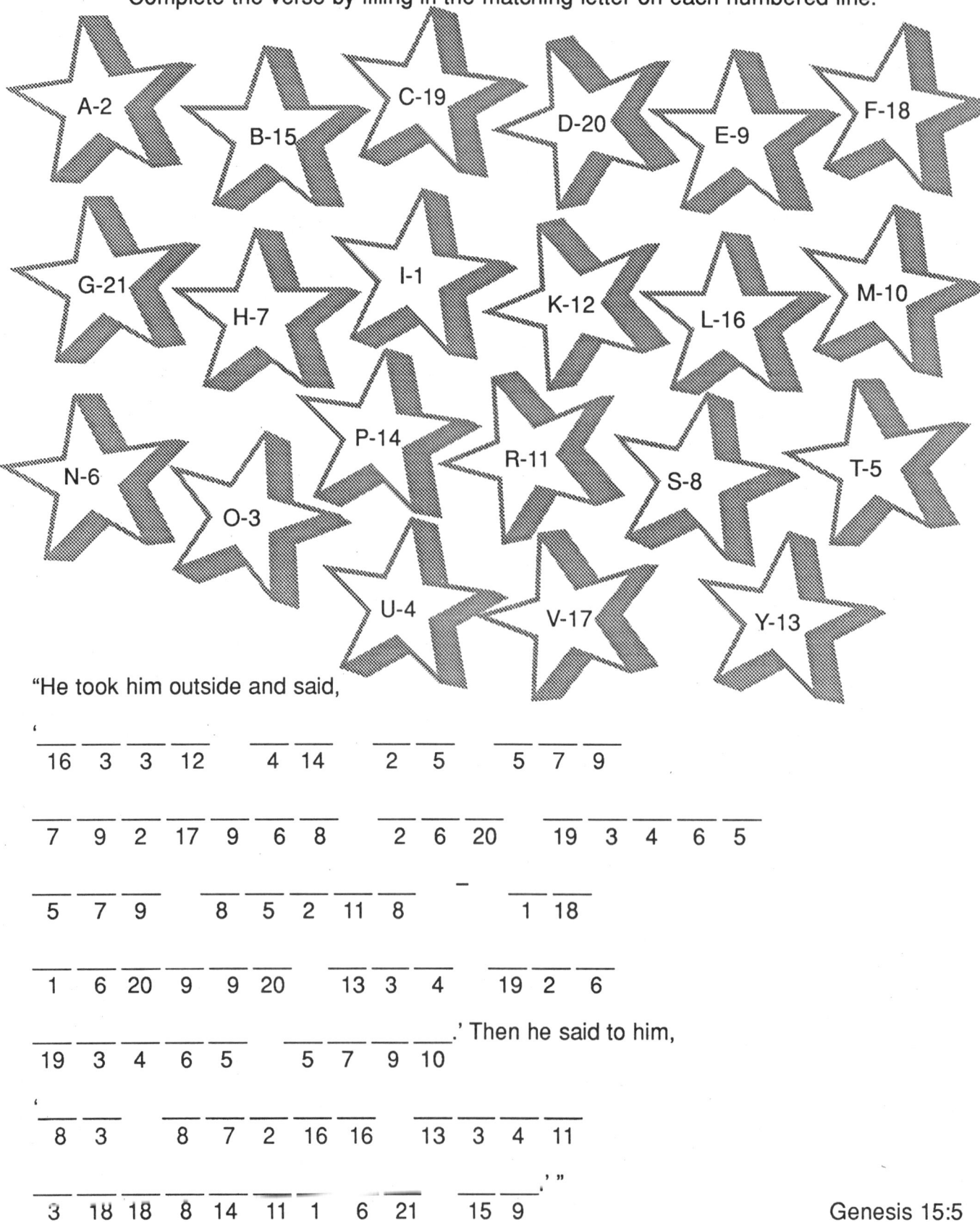

A-2, B-15, C-19, D-20, E-9, F-18, G-21, H-7, I-1, K-12, L-16, M-10, N-6, O-3, P-14, R-11, S-8, T-5, U-4, V-17, Y-13

"He took him outside and said,

'_ _ _ _ _ _ _ _ _ _ _
 16 3 3 12 4 14 2 5 5 7 9

_ _ _ _ _ _ _ _ _ _ _ _ _ _ _
7 9 2 17 9 6 8 2 6 20 19 3 4 6 5

_ _ _ _ _ _ _ _ — _ _
5 7 9 8 5 2 11 8   1 18

_ _ _ _ _ _ _ _ _ _ _ _
1 6 20 9 9 20 13 3 4 19 2 6

_ _ _ _ _   _ _ _ _.' Then he said to him,
19 3 4 6 5   5 7 9 10

'_ _ _ _ _ _ _ _ _ _ _ _
 8 3 8 7 2 16 16 13 3 4 11

_ _ _ _ _ _ _ _ _ _.'"
3 18 18 8 14 11 1 6 21 15 9

Genesis 15:5

The Visit

Find and circle the seven words.

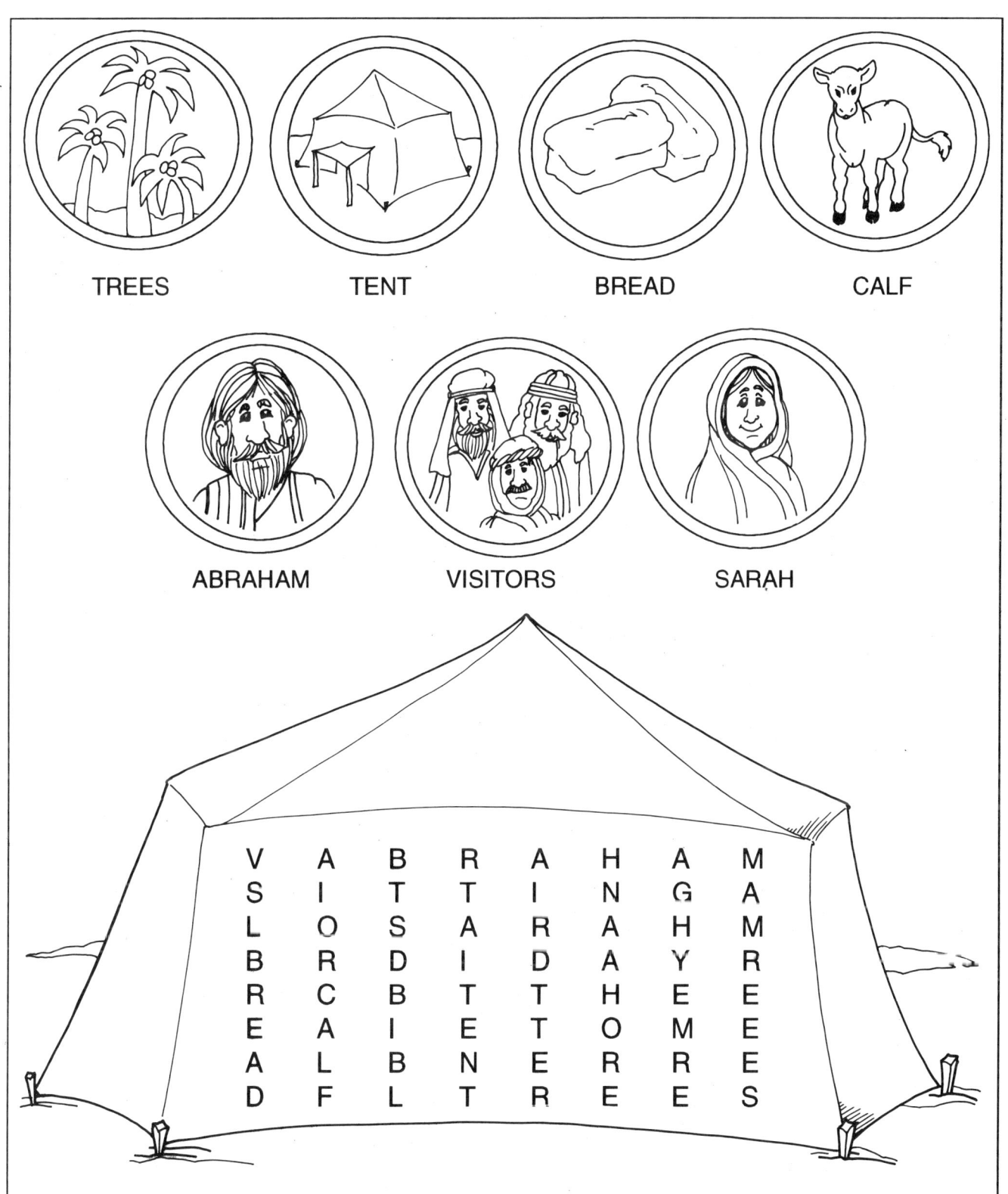

TREES TENT BREAD CALF

ABRAHAM VISITORS SARAH

V	A	B	R	A	H	A	M
S	I	T	T	I	N	G	A
L	O	S	A	R	A	H	M
B	R	D	I	D	A	Y	R
R	C	B	T	D	H	E	E
E	A	I	E	T	O	M	E
A	L	B	N	T	R	R	E
D	F	L	T	R	E	E	S

"The Lord appeared to Abraham near the great trees of Mamre while he was sitting at the entrance to his tent in the heat of the day." Genesis 18:1

A Name for Abraham's Son

Abraham gave his son a name which means "he laughs." To find the name, color the spaces according to the color code given. Then write the name in the blanks to complete the verse.

1 – BLUE   2 – ORANGE   3 – GREEN   4 – RED   5 – PURPLE   6 – YELLOW

"Abraham gave the name ___ ___ ___ ___ ___ to the son Sarah bore him."

Genesis 21:3

Rebekah at the Well

The servant took ten camels with him when he went to find a wife for Isaac. Circle ten camels in the picture below.

"So she quickly emptied her jar into the trough, ran back to the well to draw more water, and drew enough for all his camels." Genesis 24:20

Abraham/Moses Mask

Color, cut out, and laminate the mask below. To make a face mask, cut out the eyes; then punch a small hole on each side and add string or elastic. To make a stick mask, cut out the eyes. Then glue a paint stirrer or ruler to the back. To make a puppet, glue the face to a paper bag. Use the mask when putting on a presentation about Abraham or Moses.

Abraham Bible Story Patterns

Reduce or enlarge these figures for puppets, flannelboard stories, bulletin board displays, shoe box dioramas, shoe box stages, stationery, pencil toppers, storytelling, play props, or backgrounds.

ABRAHAM

SARAH

LOT

TENT

SERVANT

ALTAR

THREE VISITORS

ISAAC

REBEKAH

Shining Star Publications, Copyright © 1994

SS3840

God Blesses Abraham in Many Ways

Characters: narrator(s), Abram/Abraham, Lot, two herdsmen, chorus, Sarah, three visitors

Setting: Outdoor backdrop with hills to one side and trees to the other. A real tent can be set up near the trees.

Narrator: One day God told Abram to leave the land of his fathers and go to another land.

Chorus: Go to the land I show you.

Narrator: Abram gathered his belongings and set out with his wife, a relative named Lot, and some others. During the trip, Abram was blessed by God in many ways, and he acquired much silver, gold, and livestock. Lot also had a lot of animals. The land could not support all the camels, donkeys, sheep, and cattle that they both had.

Herdsman 1: (Running in) Abram! Abram! We just had another quarrel with Lot's herdsmen. We found a good piece of land for grazing, but Lot's herdsmen claim they found it first.

Herdsman 2: There's simply not enough food here for all your animals and Lot's too. You must do something.

Abram: I'll go to see him at once. (Walks across the stage toward Lot)

Lot: Hello, Abram. What brings you here today?

Abram: It's our herdsmen, Lot. They've been fighting over grazing land. I do not want bad feelings between us or between our herdsmen. There is much more land out there. Let's separate. You head out toward the area of land you want. Then I will go the other way.

Lot: It's very kind of you to give me first choice.

Lot, Abram, and Chorus: "Abram and Lot's Song"

Narrator: So Lot and Abram parted. Lot set out to the east. Abram moved his tents and went to live near the great trees of Mamre where he built an altar to the Lord. (Abram piles up a few rocks or blocks.) Some time later, God spoke to him. He told Abram to look up to the heavens and count the stars, for his descendants would be as numerous as the stars.

Chorus: "Look Up High and Count Each Star"

Narrator: When Abram was ninety-nine years old, the Lord spoke to him again. He told Abram that from then on he would be called Abraham, which means Father of Many. Sarai, his wife, would be called Sarah, for she would have a son the next year and would become the mother of many nations. Abraham wondered about all he had been told.

Abraham: Will I really have a son when I am one hundred, and will Sarah have a child at the age of ninety? How is it possible? We are so old.

Chorus: "Can Abraham Still Have a Son?"

Narrator: Not long after that, Abraham was sitting at the entrance to his tent when he saw three visitors. Abraham knew they were not ordinary visitors, so he got up and bowed before them.

Abraham: (Bowing down) Please, Lord, do not pass me by. Rest under this tree and let me get you some water to wash your feet and some food to eat.

Visitor 1: Very well. Do as you say.

Abraham: (Talking into tent) Sarah, quick! Make some bread for our visitors, and I will have a servant prepare a calf for them to eat.

Narrator: So a meal was prepared for the visitors.

Abraham: Here is some food and milk for you (handing food to the three).

Visitor 2: Where is your wife, Sarah?

Abraham: She is inside the tent.

Visitor 3: I will return at this time next year, and Sarah will have a son.

Sarah: (From inside the tent) Hee, hee, hee. A son at my age!

Chorus: "Sarah's Laughter"

Narrator: Sarah and Abraham had a son the next year just as the Lord had said. They named him Isaac, which means "he laughs."

Sarah: God has brought me laughter, and everyone who hears that I gave Abraham a son in his old age will laugh with me.

Narrator: So God blessed Abraham with a son.

Chorus: Abraham's descendants became too numerous to count, like the stars in the heavens. Abraham became a father to many.

Chorus: "Father Abraham Had Many Sons"
(This well-known chorus is not included in this book.)

Songs Sung New

Go to the Land
Tune: "Go Tell Aunt Rhodie"

Go to the land I show you.
Go to the land I show you.
Go to the land I show you.
Leave your father's home.

Abram and Lot's Song
Tune: "Did You Ever See a Lassie?"

The more we stay together,
Together, together,
The more we stay together
The harder it will be.

For your flocks and my flocks
Keep getting much larger.
The more we stay together
The harder it will be.

The more we stay together,
Together, together,
The more we stay together
The harder it will be.

For your herds and my herds
Keep getting much larger.
The more we stay together
The harder it will be.

The more we stay together,
Together, together,
The more we stay together
The harder it will be.

For your men fight my men
And my men fight your men.
The more we stay together
The harder it will be.

Look Up High and Count Each Star
Tune: "Twinkle, Twinkle, Little Star"

Look up high and count each star.
See how many stars there are.
Like the stars your numbers will be.
Just be patient, you will see.
Look up high and count each star.
See how many stars there are.

Can Abraham Still Have a Son?
Tune: "Do You Know the Muffin Man?"

Can Abraham still have a son,
Still have a son, still have a son?
Can Abraham still have a son
Though he's growing old?

Yes, Abraham can have a son,
Can have a son, can have a son.
Yes, Abraham can have a son
With the Lord God's blessing.

Can Sarah have a child,
Have a child, have a child?
Can Sarah have a child
Though she's growing old?

Yes, Sarah can have a child,
Can have a child, can have a child.
Yes, Sarah can have a child
With the Lord God's blessing.

Sarah's Laughter
Tune: "Jingle Bells"

Ha, ha, ha! Hee, hee, hee!
Ha, ha, ha, hee, hee!
I just heard a most absurd
Thing will happen to me-ee.
Ha, ha, ha! Hee, hee, hee!
Ha, ha, ha, hee, hee!
How can I believe at my old age
A son will be born to me?

Abraham's Picture Game

Cut out the picture squares and the star squares on the next page. Arrange the pictures in any order on the game card below. When the leader calls out a picture, cover it with a star. The winner is the first one to get four stars in a row. Give star stickers for prizes.

"He took him outside and said, 'Look up at the heavens and count the stars – if indeed you can count them.' Then he said to him, 'So shall your offspring be.' " Genesis 15:5

Abraham's Picture Game

Cut out the picture squares and the stars below and use them to play Abraham's Picture Game on page 21.

Shining Star Publications, Copyright © 1994 — SS3840

Abraham Art

Decorate a room or table with these projects, and invite others to your Bible hero "museum."

Mobile of Many Blessings
Make a mobile showing some of Abraham's blessings. Then make a mobile of blessings God has given you.

"Your Name Will Be Abraham"
Lightly trace a coloring book picture of Abraham or the pattern on page 17. Use fine-point markers or colored pencils to write the word *Abraham* over and over along his outline. You may want to use different colors for different sections.

Stars, Stars
Draw a star 2" or 3" wide on a piece of heavy paper and cut it out. Trace the star pattern over and over with different colors on a sheet of white paper. Overlap the stars to create a beautiful design. At the bottom of the paper, write the words of Genesis 15:5.

Landscape Art
Use paint, chalk, or markers to make a landscape scene of one of the locations (Egypt, hills east of Bethel, trees of Mamre, etc.) mentioned in the Bible story of Abraham.

Father of Many Nations
Cut out the letters A-B-R-A-H-A-M. Each letter should be at least 12" high. Put the letters on a bulletin board along with the words of Genesis 17:5. Everyone can cut out faces of many nationalities of people from old magazines or draw children in international costumes to display on or around the large letters.

Shining Star Publications, Copyright © 1994   SS3840

The Story of Joseph

A Story Based on Genesis 37; 39–45

(Note: Use the patterns on pages 25, 35, and 38 to create flannelboard pieces, stick puppets, or play props to emphasize the underlined words of the story.)

Once there was a man named Jacob who had many sons. One of the sons was named Joseph. Jacob loved Joseph best and made him a fine robe. This made Joseph's older brothers angry. They became angrier still when Joseph told them about his dreams. In one dream the brothers were working in the field when suddenly their sheaves of grain bowed to Joseph's sheaf of grain. In another dream, the sun, the moon, and eleven stars bowed to Joseph. Did this mean Joseph's family would one day bow to him?

One day when the brothers were watching their father's sheep, Jacob sent Joseph to check on them. The brothers saw Joseph coming and came up with a plan to get rid of him. The brothers took off the fine robe Joseph had on; then they threw him into an empty well. They planned to leave him in the well, but soon some merchants came by, so they took him out of the well and sold him. Then they dipped his robe in blood and took it back to Jacob. Jacob was very sad when he saw the robe. He thought Joseph had been killed by a wild animal.

Meanwhile, Joseph was taken to Egypt where he was sold as a slave. One day Joseph was accused of something he didn't do, and he was thrown into prison. While he was in prison, two other prisoners told their dreams to him. One prisoner had been Pharaoh's cupbearer; the other had been Pharaoh's baker. Joseph was able to tell both men the meaning of their dreams. He said that in three days the cupbearer would be released and would work for Pharaoh once again. The baker would be put to death. Everything happened just as Joseph had said.

Two years later, Pharaoh had a dream which no one in the palace could interpret. The cupbearer told Pharaoh about Joseph, who was still in prison. When Pharaoh heard that Joseph could interpret dreams, he had Joseph brought to him.

Joseph listened as Pharaoh told him about his dream. In it, seven healthy cows had been swallowed by seven scrawny ones, and seven healthy heads of grain had been swallowed by seven withered ones. Joseph said that there would be seven years when food would be plentiful in the land. Then there would be seven years of famine. Joseph said that grain from the good years should be stored so there would be food to eat during the years of famine.

Pharaoh saw that Joseph was wise and that he had found favor with God. He put Joseph in charge of the land and the storage of grain. When the years of famine came, people from other lands came to Joseph to buy food. Even Joseph's brothers came and bowed before him, though they did not recognize him. The second time his brothers came to buy grain, Joseph revealed himself to them. The brothers were frightened and upset, but Joseph told them not to be afraid. He said everything that had happened was part of God's plan to save lives. After Joseph gave his brothers many gifts, he sent them back to Canaan to get Jacob. When Jacob found out that Joseph was still alive, he was filled with joy.

Celebrating Joseph

Joseph Jubilations

1. To create a Joseph costume, cut holes in a pillowcase for head and arms. Decorate with beads, sequins, drawings, etc. Everyone can perform Joseph songs in the "robes."

2. Have a Food-a-Plenty Day. Bring some of your food out of storage to give to a poor family, or prepare a meal for someone. Things to serve might include the cupbearer's grapes, the baker's bread, and grain items such as cereal.

3. Have a Joseph Jamboree. Pass out copies of Joseph songs, page 39, for everyone to sing. Have a table of material scraps, sequins, etc., for contestants to use in an ornamented robe contest. Think of some Joseph carnival games to play. For example, put a cardboard picture of Joseph, backed with a magnet, in a large tub. Blindfold players, give them strings with magnets attached, and allow them fifteen seconds to try to fish Joseph out of the "well."

4. Use the patterns in this unit for jobs well-done or add them to the top of heavy strips of paper to create Bible bookmarks.

5. Use the certificate on the right as an invitation to your Food-a-Plenty Day, Joseph Jamboree, or play. Use it as an award for a star performance, a reward for completion of the Joseph activity sheets, a take-home memory verse card, a thank-you note, or as a record sheet of Joseph stories read.

Shining Star Publications, Copyright © 1994   25   SS3840

Jealous Brothers

One day Joseph's brothers took his robe off and threw him into a well. Later, they pulled him out and sold him as a slave.

2

Joseph's Robe

Joseph's father, Jacob, made him a beautiful robe. This made his brothers jealous.

1

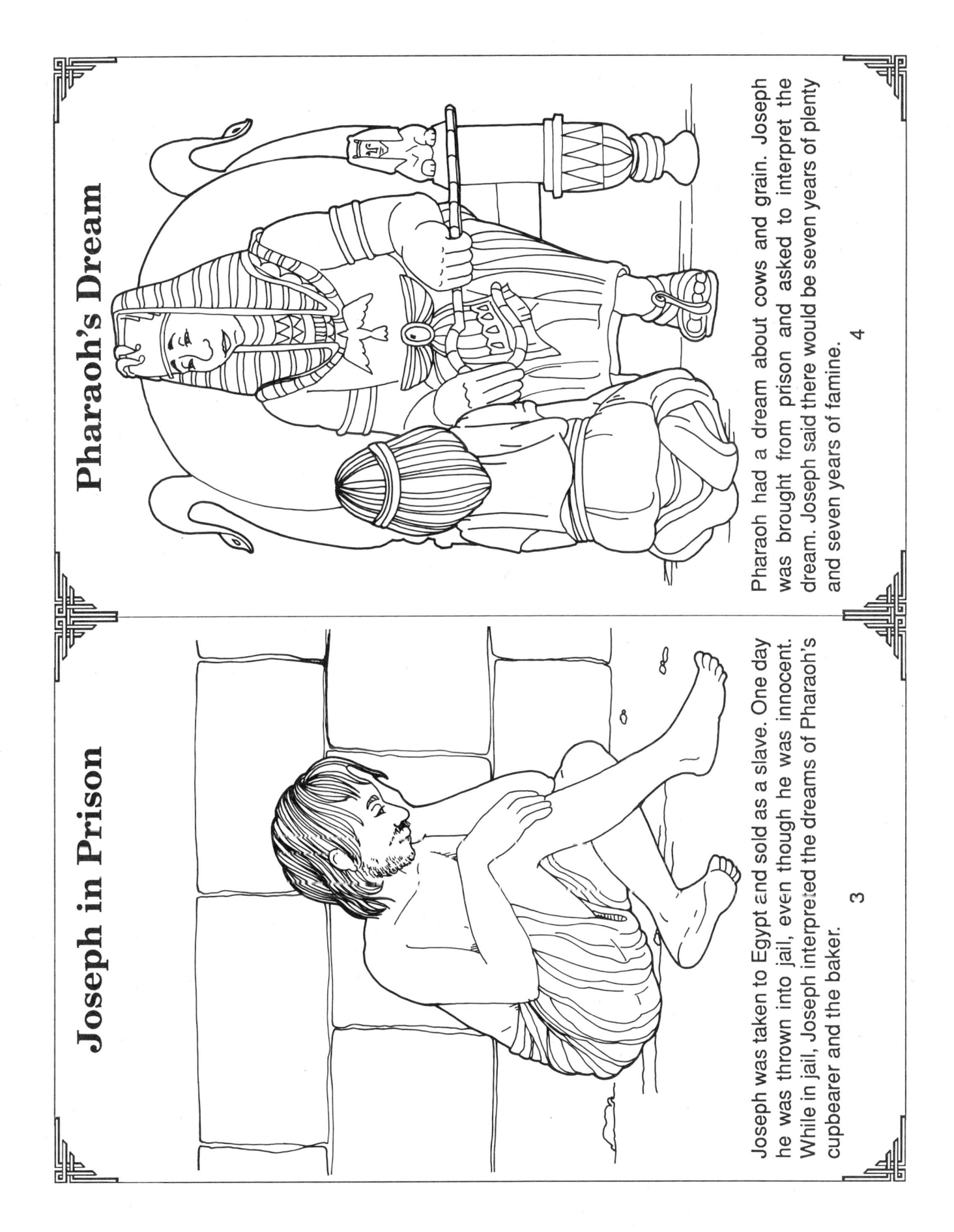

Pharaoh's Dream

Pharaoh had a dream about cows and grain. Joseph was brought from prison and asked to interpret the dream. Joseph said there would be seven years of plenty and seven years of famine.

4

Joseph in Prison

Joseph was taken to Egypt and sold as a slave. One day he was thrown into jail, even though he was innocent. While in jail, Joseph interpreted the dreams of Pharaoh's cupbearer and the baker.

3

Abraham's Request

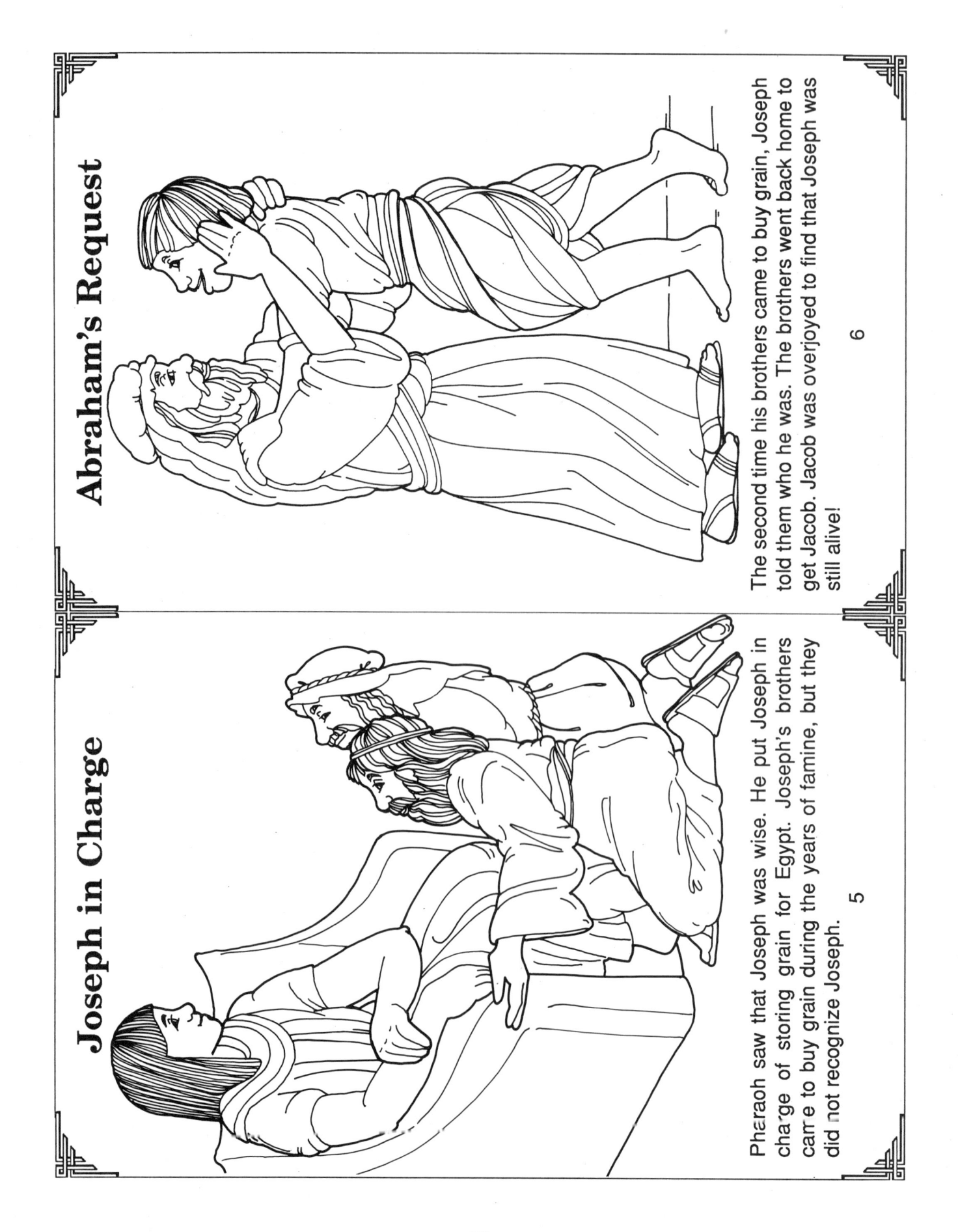

The second time his brothers came to buy grain, Joseph told them who he was. The brothers went back home to get Jacob. Jacob was overjoyed to find that Joseph was still alive!

6

Joseph in Charge

Pharaoh saw that Joseph was wise. He put Joseph in charge of storing grain for Egypt. Joseph's brothers came to buy grain during the years of famine, but they did not recognize Joseph.

5

Shining Star Publications, Copyright © 1994

SS3840

Joseph's Robe

Color the pair of matching robes alike.

"Now Israel loved Joseph more than any of his other sons, because he had been born to him in his old age; and he made a richly ornamented robe for him."

Genesis 37:3

Pulled from a Well

Circle ten ways the bottom picture is different from the top one.

"So when the Midianite merchants came by, his brothers pulled Joseph up out of the cistern and sold him for twenty shekels of silver to the Ishmaelites, who took him to Egypt."
Genesis 37:28

The Cupbearer and the Baker

Circle the key words in the puzzle.

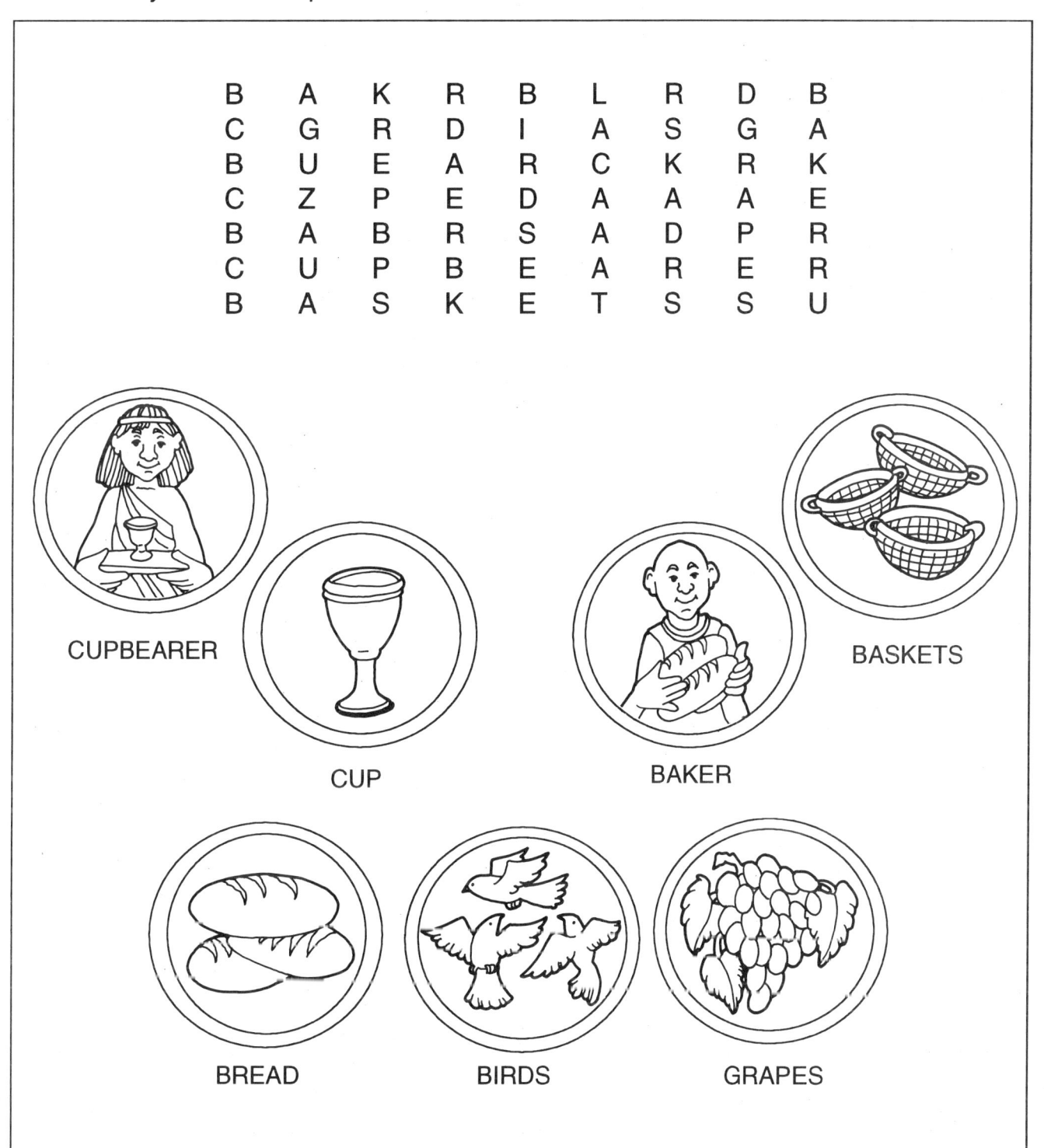

```
B A K R B L R D B
C G R D I A S G A
B U E A R C K R K
C Z P E D A A A E
B A B R S A D P R
C U P B E A R E R
B A S K E T S S U
```

CUPBEARER   CUP   BAKER   BASKETS

BREAD   BIRDS   GRAPES

" . . . After they had been in custody for some time, each of the two men – the cupbearer and the baker of the king of Egypt, who were being held in prison – had a dream the same night, and each dream had a meaning of its own."

Genesis 40:4-5

Interpreting Pharaoh's Dream

Pharaoh's dream was filled with symbols. God made their meaning clear through Joseph. Fill in the matching letters for the symbols to find out the meaning of Pharaoh's dream.

A	!	E	%	I	(	O	<	T	¢	Y	÷
B	@	F	^	L	)	P	>	U	ø		
C	#	G	&	M	+	R	?	V	~		
D	$	H	*	N	=	S	'	W	–		

"Seven years of great abundance are coming throughout the land of Egypt, but seven years of famine will follow them."

Genesis 41:29-30a

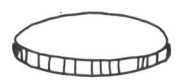

Hidden Silver

Joseph's brothers did not know they were returning home with the silver they had brought as payment for their grain. Circle ten silver coins hidden in the picture below.

"Joseph gave orders to fill their bags with grain, to put each man's silver back in his sack, and to give them provisions for their journey." Genesis 42:25a

Joseph and His Brothers

After you hear the story of Joseph and his brothers from Genesis 45, underline the correct answer for each clue. Then use the answers to fill in the crossword puzzle.

ACROSS

4. What Joseph gave all his brothers (CLOTHING, EMERALDS, JEWELRY)
6. What Joseph did after revealing himself to his brothers (FLED, WEPT, DIED)
7. What God sent Joseph to Egypt to save (LIVES, MONEY, BAKER)

DOWN

1. Whom Joseph sent for (FATHER, MOTHER, UNCLES)
2. Brother to whom Joseph gave most gifts (BENJAMIN, ISSACHAR, MATTHEW)
3. Joseph sent his father provisions loaded on these. (DONKEYS, CANINES, CAMELS)
4. Pharaoh told Joseph to send these for the wives and children. (PLANE, CARTS, SLEDS)
5. When Joseph revealed himself to his brothers, there were still this many years of famine to come. (NINE, FOUR, FIVE)

Shining Star Publications, Copyright © 1994   SS3840

Pharaoh Mask

Color, cut out, and laminate the mask below. To make a face mask, cut out the eyes, punch a small hole on each side, and add string or elastic. To make a stick mask, cut out the eyes and glue a paint stirrer or ruler to the back. To make a puppet, attach the head to a paper bag. Use the mask or puppet when putting on a presentation. Cut off the face, attach it to a paper headband, and wear it to a biblical feast. You may also use this mask with the Moses story.

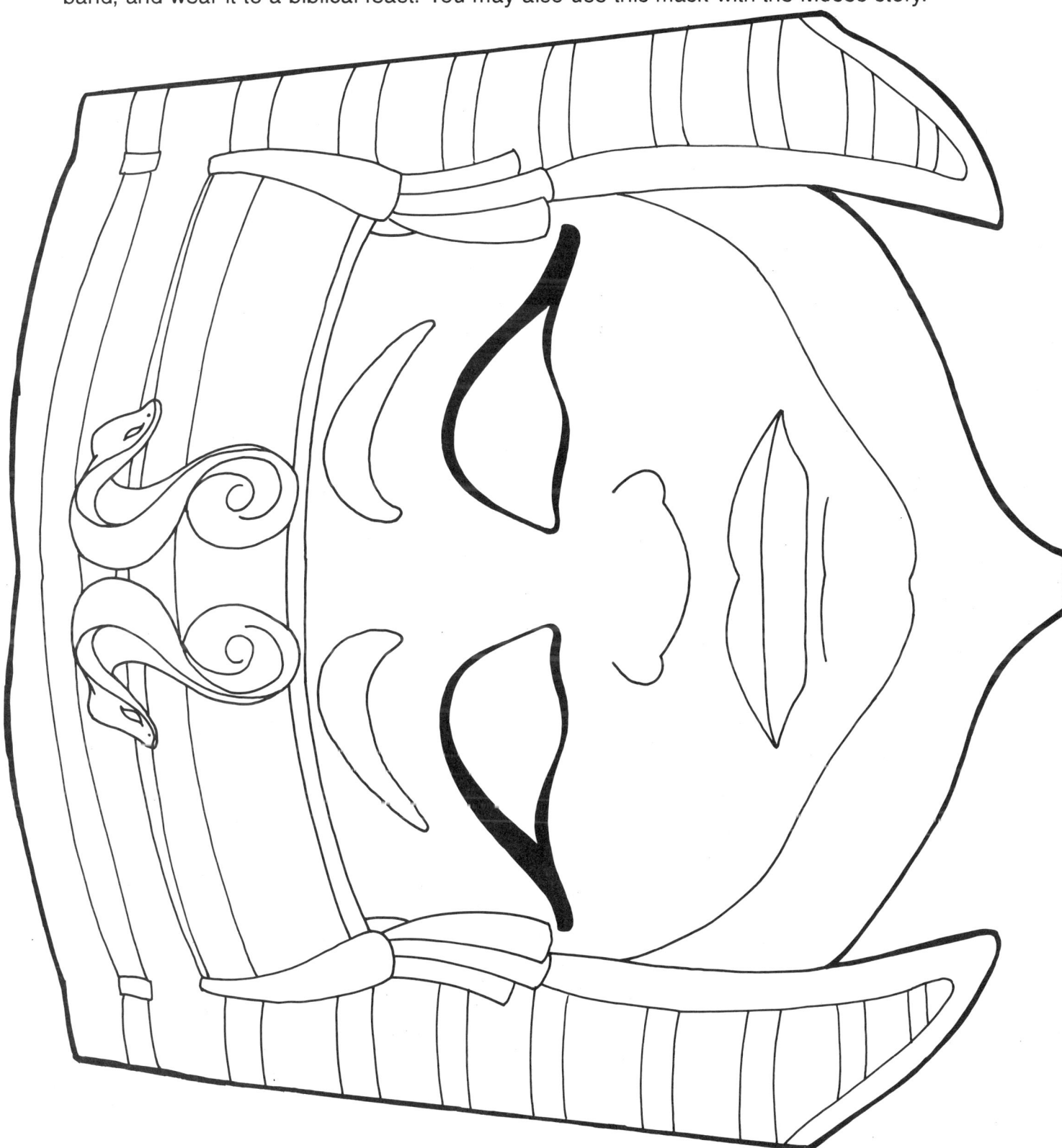

Shining Star Publications, Copyright © 1994

SS3840

Joseph's Jazzy Jacket
An Ancient Tale Told in a Modern Tongue

Characters: Narrator(s), chorus, Joseph, Jacob, brothers, merchants, cupbearer, baker, Pharaoh

Setting: A backdrop with fields and sheep at the center, a cardboard-box prison on one side, and a fancy chair on the other side

Narrator: Once there was a young man named Joseph. His father made him a fine robe. (Jacob hands Joseph a robe.) This made his brothers jealous.

Chorus: "Joseph Had a Colored Coat" (Verse 1)

Narrator: The colorful coat made Joseph's brothers think some colorful thoughts.

Brother 1: (Wearing blue) Father must love Joseph best. I feel so *blue*.

Brother 2: (Wearing green) I wish I had a fine coat. I'm *green* with envy.

Brother 3: (Wearing red) This is more than I can take. That coat makes me see *red*!

Narrator: Soon Joseph's jazzy jacket made the brothers think *black* thoughts. They looked for a chance to get even with him, especially after Joseph told them his dream.

Joseph: I had a dream that your sheaves of grain bowed to mine.

Brother 4: Do you think that means we will one day bow to you? Ha! In your dreams, brother, in your dreams.

Narrator: Then Joseph had another dream.

Joseph: I had a dream that the sun, the moon, and eleven stars were bowing to me.

Narrator: Would his father and mother and eleven brothers one day bow to Joseph? Needless to say, his brothers weren't happy after hearing about Joseph's latest dream. (Pause) One day when the brothers were watching over their father's sheep, they looked up and saw Joseph coming.

Brother 5: Here comes that dreamer, and I have a nightmare planned for him. Listen up. (Brothers gather in a huddle. When Joseph gets near, they take off his robe and throw him into a pit.)

Brother 6: That takes care of him. Let's sit down and have a bite to eat. (All but Reuben sit down and begin to take out cartons and bags labeled Dothan Doughnuts, Canaan Cheese, Camel Milk, etc.)

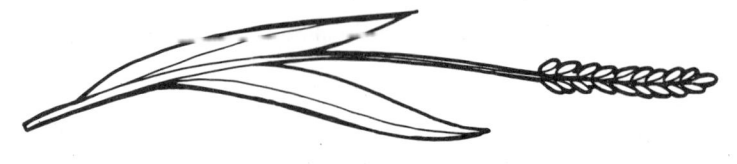

Shining Star Publications, Copyright © 1994

SS3840

Brother 7: (As Reuben walks off) Reuben, where are you going?

Brother 8: To get a Reuben sandwich, of course! (Exits)

Brother 9: (Pointing as merchants enter) Look, merchants!

Brother 10: I think the idea of leaving Joseph in that pit is the pits. Let's sell him instead to the merchants and divvy up the silver.

Several Brothers: Yeah, that sounds great!

Narrator: So the brothers sold Joseph. (Merchants pay and take Joseph away.) Then they put blood on his fine coat and took it to Jacob, who thought his son must have been killed by a wild animal. (Brothers give Jacob the coat.)

Chorus: "A Coat That Was Oh, So Fine"

Narrator: Meanwhile, Joseph was sold in Egypt as a slave. One day he was falsely accused and thrown into prison. Pharaoh's chief baker and his cupbearer were assigned to the same prison as Joseph. Each had a dream he did not understand.

Chorus: "Who Can Tell?" (Cupbearer verse and chorus)

Cupbearer: In my dream I saw a vine with three branches. Soon the vine was full of grapes which I took and squeezed into Pharaoh's cup.

Song: "The Cupbearer"

Joseph: The three vines are three days. In three days Pharaoh will ask you to be his cupbearer again. Everything will go well for you. When it does, remember to tell Pharaoh about me, for I am wrongfully in prison.

Baker: I, too, had a dream. Can you tell me its meaning?

Chorus: "Who Can Tell" (Baker verse and chorus)

Baker: In my dream I was carrying three baskets of bread on my head, but the birds were eating the baked goods out of the top basket.

Chorus: "The Baker"

Joseph: The three baskets are three days. In three days Pharaoh will have you hung from a tree, and the birds will pick at your flesh.

Narrator: Everything happened just as Joseph said. Two years later Pharaoh (sitting on chair) could find no one to interpret his dreams. Then the cupbearer remembered Joseph in prison. The cupbearer told Pharaoh about Joseph, and Pharaoh sent for him. (Joseph enters.)

Pharaoh: I hear you can interpret dreams. Can you interpret mine?

Joseph: Only God can give you the answer you need.

Chorus: "Who Can Tell?" (Pharaoh verse and chorus)

Pharaoh: In one dream, seven healthy cows were grazing. Then seven skinny cows came and ate them. In another dream, I saw seven good heads of grain on a single stalk. After them came seven thin and withered ones scorched by the east wind. They swallowed up the good ones.

Chorus: "Pharaoh's Dream"

Joseph: Both dreams mean the same thing. The seven good cows and heads of grain mean there will be seven years when food will be plentiful in Egypt. After that will come seven years of famine. Some of the food from the good years should be saved for the bad years.

Pharaoh: That is a good idea. Since you are so wise and since God has made all this known to you, I will put you in charge of all the land. (Exits)

Narrator: So Joseph was put in charge of the land of Egypt. He had the people store food from the good years. During the years of famine, people came from many places to buy grain from him. Even Joseph's brothers came, though they did not recognize him. (Brothers bow at Joseph's feet.) When Joseph revealed himself to them, they were frightened at first, but Joseph forgave them. He told them not to be upset for what they had done to him, for everything had been a part of God's plan to save lives. (Brothers exit and reenter with Jacob.) The brothers brought Jacob to Egypt, and he was overjoyed to see his son Joseph alive! (Embrace)

Chorus: "Joseph Had a Colored Coat"

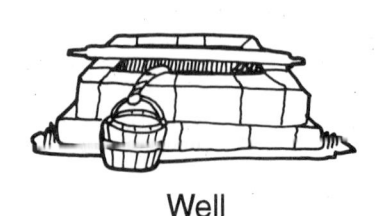

Joseph   Brothers

Jacob   Well   Birds

Songs Sung New

Joseph Had a Colored Coat
Tune: "Head and Shoulders, Knees, and Toes"

Joseph had a colored coat, colored coat.
Joseph had a colored coat, colored coat.
And that jacket got his brothers' goat.
Joseph had a colored coat, colored coat.

All that happened was God's plan, was God's plan.
All that happened was God's plan, was God's plan.
God chose Joseph to save lives in the land.
All that happened was God's plan, was God's plan.

Who Can Tell?
Tune: "Do You Know the Muffin Man"

Who can tell the cupbearer,
The cupbearer, the cupbearer?
Who can tell the cupbearer
The meaning of his dream?

Chorus:
Only God through Joseph can,
Through Joseph can, through Joseph can.
Only God through Joseph can
Tell him what it means.

Who can tell the baker man,
The baker man, the baker man?
Who can tell the baker man
The meaning of his dream?
(Chorus)

Who can tell the Pharaoh grand,
The Pharaoh grand, the Pharaoh grand?
Who can tell the Pharaoh grand
The meaning of his dream?
(Chorus)

The Cupbearer
Tune: "The Old Gray Mare"

The cupbearer, he dreamed of grapes on a vine,
Dreamed of grapes on a vine, dreamed of grapes on a vine.
The cupbearer, he dreamed of grapes on a vine,
Many long years ago.

The Baker
Tune: "A Tisket, a Tasket"

A tisket, a tasket, the baker had some baskets.
A flock of birds took all the bread
From the baskets on his head.

A Coat That Was Oh, So Fine
Tune: "Joshua Fought the Battle of Jericho"

Jacob made a coat that was oh, so fine,
Oh, so fine, oh, so fine.
Jacob made a coat that was oh, so fine,
And he gave that coat to Joseph.

Joseph wore the coat that was oh, so fine,
Oh, so fine, oh, so fine.
Joseph wore the coat that was oh, so fine,
And it made his brothers angry.

Brothers took the coat that was oh, so fine,
Oh, so fine, oh, so fine.
Brothers took the coat that was oh, so fine,
And they dipped that coat in blood.

Jacob saw the coat that was oh, so fine,
Oh, so fine, oh, so fine.
Jacob saw the coat that was oh, so fine,
And he wept for his poor son.

*Pharaoh's Dream
Tune: "This Old Man"

Pharaoh dreamed of cow one,
Grazing in the bright warm sun. (Chorus)

Pharaoh dreamed of cow two,
It had lots of grass to chew. (Chorus)

Pharaoh dreamed of cow three,
Lying underneath a tree. (Chorus)

Pharaoh dreamed of cow four,
It kept eating more and more. (Chorus)

Pharaoh dreamed of cow five,
Healthy, strong and much alive. (Chorus)

Pharaoh dreamed of cow six,
Free of sickness, free of ticks. (Chorus)

Pharaoh dreamed of cow seven,
It was a sign sent from heaven. (Chorus)

Chorus:
Along came another cow,
Thin, ugly, and weak,
That swallowed up
That cow so sleek.

*(First published in *The Stories of Noah and Joseph*, Shining Star Publications)

Saving for the Famine

Cut out the markers and the grain cards on page 41. Pile the grain cards in the middle of the gameboard. Each player selects a numbered marker and places it on any blank gameboard space. Players take turns rolling a die and moving clockwise around the gameboard the number of spaces indicated by the die. Whenever a player lands on a grain space, the player takes a grain card. When all grain cards have been collected, the game ends. The player with the most grain cards wins the game.

Saving for the Famine

Color and cut out the markers and grain cards. Use them to play the game, "Saving for the Famine," on page 40.

| 1 | 2 | 3 | 4 | 5 | 6 |

An Ornamented Coat

Color and cut out the coat and ornaments. Back the coat with cardboard. Decorate it with the ornaments.

The Story of Moses

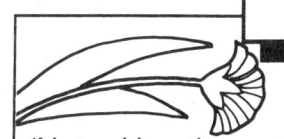

A Story Based on Exodus 1–14

(Note: Use the patterns on pages 16, 35, 44, and 54-55 to create flannelboard pieces, stick puppets, or play props to emphasize the underlined words of the story.)

Long ago a cruel <u>Pharaoh</u>, or king, ruled over Egypt. He made the Hebrew people work as <u>slaves</u>. Some were forced to make bricks and build cities for the <u>Pharaoh</u>. Others had to work long hours in the fields. Though they were made to work hard, the Hebrews grew in number. This made the <u>Pharaoh</u> angry. He was afraid that one day the Hebrews would outnumber the Egyptians and rise up against them. So he ordered that all Hebrew baby boys be thrown into the Nile <u>River</u>.

One Hebrew mother made a special <u>basket</u> and put her baby boy inside. She set the <u>basket</u> among the reeds along the banks of the Nile <u>River</u>. The baby's <u>sister</u> watched from a distance to see what would happen. Soon the Pharaoh's daughter, the <u>princess</u>, came to the <u>river</u> to bathe. She spotted the <u>basket</u> among the reeds and sent her maid to fetch it. When the <u>princess</u> saw the baby inside, she felt sorry for him. Seeing that the <u>princess</u> loved the baby, his <u>sister</u> stepped forward and offered to find someone to help care for him. The <u>princess</u> accepted the offer, and the baby's own mother got to care for the baby while he was young. When the boy grew older, he was taken to the palace; and the <u>princess</u> raised him as her son. She named him Moses, which means "drawn from the water."

When <u>Moses</u> grew up, he helped a Hebrew slave who was being mistreated by an Egyptian. This made the <u>Pharaoh</u> angry. <u>Moses</u> feared for his life and ran away to another land where he became a shepherd.

One day, while <u>Moses</u> was tending sheep, God spoke to him from a <u>burning</u> <u>bush</u>. He told <u>Moses</u> to lead the Hebrew people, the Israelites, out of Egypt. <u>Moses</u> and his brother, <u>Aaron</u>, went to the <u>Pharaoh</u> and asked him to let the Israelites go. To show that they had been sent by God, <u>Aaron</u> threw his staff on the ground and it became a <u>snake</u>.

<u>Pharaoh</u> would not listen, so God sent many <u>plagues</u>, or hardships, upon Egypt. For example, <u>frogs</u> came up onto the land and into the houses of the Egyptians, the livestock grew sick, <u>flies</u> swarmed everywhere, <u>locusts</u> ate the crops, and the firstborn male in every Egyptian household died.

Finally, <u>Pharaoh</u> let the Israelites go. But once they were gone, <u>Pharaoh</u> was sorry he no longer had them as slaves. He ordered his <u>soldiers</u> to bring the Israelites back again. When the <u>soldiers</u> caught up with the Israelites at the Red <u>Sea</u>, <u>Moses</u> stretched out his staff and God parted the <u>sea</u> so that the Israelites could cross safely on dry ground. Then God made the <u>sea</u> flow back into place so that the Egyptian <u>soldiers</u> could not follow. The Israelites were safe at last, and <u>Moses</u> was a hero!

Celebrating Moses

Moses Merriment

1. Create a Moses mobile of plagues or of Exodus scenes. Then complete some of the other art projects in this unit and invite others to your Museum of Moses Masterpieces.

2. Learn about foods of Moses' time. Plan a menu of "Moses Morsels." Write the menu on stone-shaped paper tablets. Serve a Moses meal to parents, invalids, or another class.

3. Have a Pharaoh festival in which all games include an Exodus theme. For example, game participants may fish from the Nile; try to guess which of three baskets has baby Moses inside; or toss toy frogs, locusts, and flies into a container.

4. Use the frog or locust as a pencil topper for a job well-done, or add them to the top of heavy strips of paper to create Bible bookmarks.

5. Use the certificate above as an invitation to a Moses musical, meal, masterpiece display, or festival. Use it as an award for a star performance, completion of the Moses activity sheets, a take-home memory verse card, a thank-you note, or as a record sheet of Moses books read.

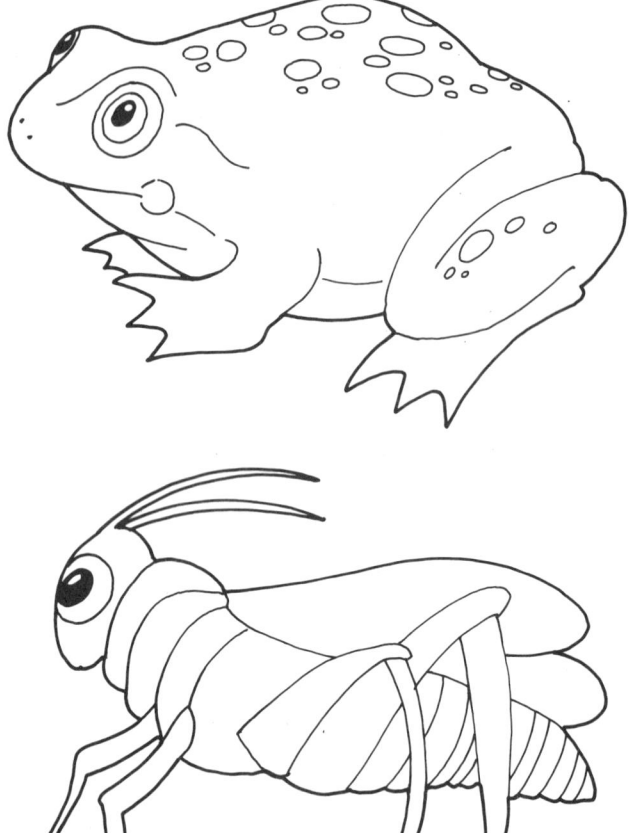

Baby Moses

One Hebrew mother put her baby boy inside a basket and set it among the reeds of the Nile River. The baby's sister watched to see what would happen.

2

Pharaoh's Command

Long ago a cruel Pharaoh ruled over Egypt. He made the Hebrew people work as slaves and ordered that all the Hebrew baby boys be thrown into the Nile River.

1

The Burning Bush

One day while Moses was tending sheep, God spoke to him from a burning bush. He told Moses to ask Pharaoh to let the Israelites go.

4

A Basket in the Reeds

Pharaoh's daughter spotted the baby and felt sorry for him. When the boy was a little older, the princess took him and raised him as her son. She named him Moses, which means "drawn from the water."

3

The Parting of the Sea

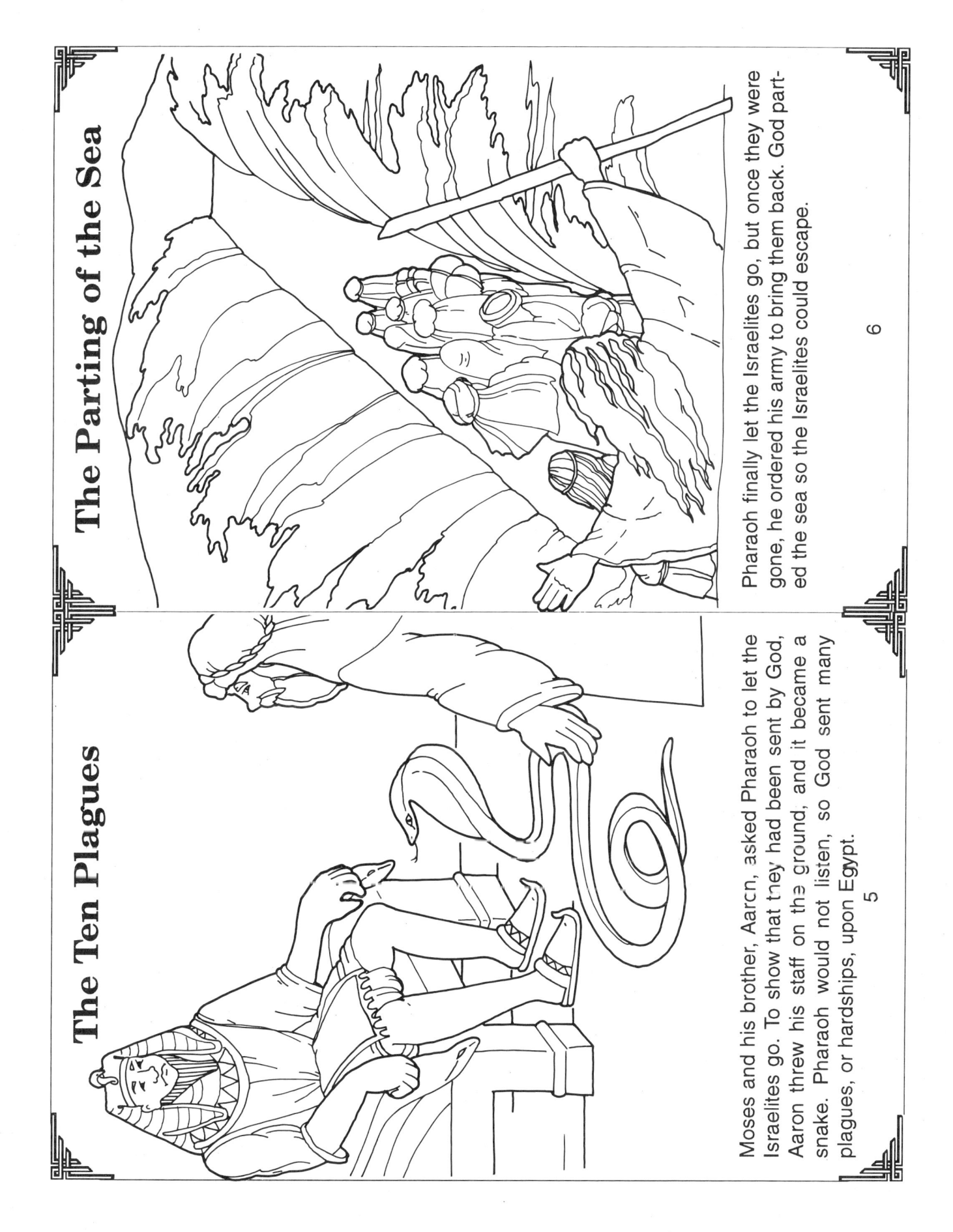

Pharaoh finally let the Israelites go, but once they were gone, he ordered his army to bring them back. God parted the sea so the Israelites could escape.

6

The Ten Plagues

Moses and his brother, Aaron, asked Pharaoh to let the Israelites go. To show that they had been sent by God, Aaron threw his staff on the ground, and it became a snake. Pharaoh would not listen, so God sent many plagues, or hardships, upon Egypt.

5

Shining Star Publications, Copyright © 1994

SS3840

Slaves, Slaves

Color the pair of matching slaves alike.

"So they put slave masters over them to oppress them with forced labor, . . ."

Exodus 1:11

Baby in a Basket

Find and circle the hidden words.

BABY

BASKET

REEDS

NILE

PRINCESS

MAID

SISTER

```
S B R E T S I S
A B A Z K R T N
M Z N S M R B I
B A B Y K E T L
P R I N C E S S
R E E D S B T L
M N I L E S Z R
```

"But when she could hide him no longer, she got a papyrus basket for him and coated it with tar and pitch. Then she placed the child in it and put it among the reeds along the bank of the Nile."

Exodus 2:3

Drawn from the Water

Circle ten ways the bottom picture is different from the top one.

God Calls Moses

Help Moses and Aaron find their way through the maze to Pharaoh.

"So now, go. I am sending you to Pharaoh to bring my people the Israelites out of Egypt."
Exodus 3:10

Frolicking Frogs

Circle ten frogs hidden in the picture below.

"The frogs will go up on you and your people and all your officials." Exodus 8:4

Crossing the Sea Crossword

After you hear the story of Crossing the Sea in Exodus 14, underline the correct answer for each clue. Then use the answers to fill in the crossword puzzle.

ACROSS

1. This guided the Israelites by day. (BIRDS, CLOUD, TREES)
4. These came off the chariots used by the Egyptian army. (BRAKES, WHEELS, REINS)
5. Pharaoh's army followed the Israelites with chariots and these. (CAMELS, HORSES, CHILDREN)
7. The Israelites went through the sea on this kind of ground. (DRY, WET, CONCRETE)

DOWN

2. The Israelites camped near here. (DESERT, FOREST, SWAMP)
3. This guided the Israelites at night. (BATS, FIRE, MOON)
4. The Lord drove the sea back with this. (RAIN, WIND, SUN)
6. Moses raised this over the sea. (STAFF, STONE, ROBE)

Princess Mask

Color, cut out, and laminate the mask below. To make a face mask, cut out the eyes, punch a small hole on each side, and add string or elastic. To make a stick mask, cut out the eyes, and glue a paint stirrer or ruler to the back. To make a puppet, attach the head to a paper bag. Use the mask or puppet when putting on a presentation, or cut off the face part, attach it to a paper headband, and wear it to a biblical feast.

Moses Bible Story Patterns

Reduce or enlarge these figures and use them for puppets, flannelboard stories, bulletin board displays, shoe box dioramas, shoe box stages, stationery, pencil toppers, storytelling, play props, or backgrounds.

ADULT MOSES

FLY

BURNING BUSH

AARON

SISTER

SNAKE

SLAVES

BASKET

SOLDIERS

RIVER/SEA

Moses Musical Revue
A Memorable "Revue" of the Ten Plagues

Characters: Slaves, Narrator(s), Moses, Aaron, Pharaoh, Ten Egyptians

Setting: Pharaoh is sitting on a chair at center stage, with Moses and Aaron standing nearby. Slaves are at stage left, possibly near an outdoor backdrop. Egyptians are off-stage to the right.

Slaves: (The slaves sing "We've Been Workin' in the Hot Sun" and pretend to make bricks while singing. Blocks or boxes may serve as bricks.)

Narrator: God spoke to Moses from a burning bush. He told Moses to go to the Egyptian Pharaoh and ask him to free the Israelites who were being used as slaves.

Slaves: (Sing "Moses Had to Let the Pharaoh Know")

Narrator: Moses and his brother, Aaron, went to Pharaoh. They told him Egypt would suffer many hardships if the Israelites were not set free.

Moses and Aaron: (Sing "Pharaoh, Pharaoh." Exit)

Narrator: But Pharaoh would not listen, so Egypt was hit with the first plague.

Egyptian 1: (Enters and speaks to Pharaoh) The Nile has turned to blood! There are dead fish everywhere. Oh, what are we going to do? (Plugging nose) Something fishy is going on here. (Exits)

Narrator: Then came the second plague.

Egyptian 2: (Enters and speaks to Pharaoh) There are frogs everywhere – in my bed, in my food, even in my clothes! (Exits)

Narrator: Soon there was a third plague because Pharaoh would not listen.

Egyptian 3: (Enters and speaks to Pharaoh) There are gnats everywhere. There's even one in my hat. (Pretending to swish away gnats) Missed it! There it goes. I hope the gnat in the hat does not come back. (Exits)

Narrator: God sent a fourth plague.

Egyptian 4: (Enters) Shoo! Shoo! Shoo, fly! Don't bother me. What's with all these flies? (Looking down into a bowl) Yuck! There's even a fly in my soup . . . and this is no joke!

Narrator: Then Egypt was hit with a fifth plague.

Egyptian 5: (Enters and speaks to Pharaoh) My cattle are sick, and my goats and sheep are sick too. (Petting paper or stuffed lamb) Oh, poor little lamb. Open wide and say baa.

Moses and Aaron: (Enter before Pharaoh) Now will you let the Israelites go?

Pharaoh: No way! Get lost! (Moses and Aaron exit.)

Narrator: A sixth plague occurred.

Egyptian 6: (Enters before Pharaoh) I'm covered with boils. Oh, the pain, the pain!

Moses and Aaron: (Enter and sing "You Better Give Up")

Pharaoh: Take a hike! (Moses and Aaron exit again.)

Egyptian 7: (Enters holding up golf balls) This hail is the size of golf balls. It's destroying our roofs. (Pointing up toward imaginary roof) Why, look! There's even a "hole in one."

Moses and Aaron: Surely you're ready to let God's people go now.

Pharaoh: Nope. Now disappear. (Moses and Aaron exit.)

Narrator: Some people never learn! Plague eight was on its way.

Egyptian 8: (Entering before Pharaoh) These locusts are really bugging me. They're eating me out of house and home. (Exits)

Narrator: The ninth plague left the Egyptians in the dark as to what was happening.

Egyptian 9: (Enters and looks upward) When will these dark clouds roll away? There seems to be no end in sight. Oh, give me a home where the buffalo roam and the deer and the antelope play, where seldom is heard a discouraging word and the skies are NOT cloudy all day. (Exits)

Narrator: There was one more plague to come, the worst yet! And it was no laughing matter.

Egyptian 10: I can't believe it! My oldest son is dead. When will Pharaoh realize what he's doing to us?

Narrator: After the firstborn son in every Egyptian household died, Pharaoh finally told Moses to take the Israelites and go. After they were gone, Pharaoh changed his mind and sent his army after them. But then that's another story.

All: (Sing "Once the Lord God Sent Some Plagues")

Songs Sung New

We've Been Workin' in the Hot Sun
Tune: "I've Been Workin' on the Railroad"

We've been workin' in the hot sun
All the livelong day.
We've been makin' bricks and mortar
And yet we get no pay.
Can't you see how hard we're workin',
Laborin' for free?
Can't you see how hard we're treated?
When will we be free?

Pharaoh, let us go. Pharaoh, let us go.
Pharaoh, let us go from Egypt land.
Pharaoh, let us go. Pharaoh, let us go.
Pharaoh, let us go right now.

Someone's in the palace with Pharaoh.
Someone's in the palace we know-ow-ow-ow.
Someone's in the palace with Pharaoh
Askin' him to let us all go.

And it's Moses, Moses we know,
Moses, Moses, we know-ow-ow-ow,
Moses, Moses we know,
Askin' him to let us all go.

Pharaoh, Pharaoh
Tune: "Twinkle, Twinkle, Little Star"

Pharaoh, Pharaoh, don't you know
You must let God's people go?
If you don't you'll have to pay.
God will send ten plagues your way.
Pharaoh, Pharaoh, don't you know
You must let God's people go?

Pharaoh, God will raise His hand
And bring hardships to your land.
Ruined water, frogs, and gnats,
Other things much worse than that.
Flies, sick cattle, sores, and hail,
Locusts, darkness, doomed first males.

Pharaoh, God will raise His hand
And bring hardships to your land.

You Better Give Up
Tune: "Santa Claus Is Coming to Town"

You better give up and do what we say;
You better let the Hebrews be on their way.
God is sending more plagues your way.

Once the Lord God Sent Some Plagues
Tune: "Old McDonald Had a Farm"

Once the Lord God sent some plagues to
  E-G-Y-P-T.
And He made the river red in E-G-Y-P-T
With a fish, fish here and a fish, fish there.
Here a fish. There a fish.
Everywhere a fish, fish.
Once the Lord God sent some plagues to
  E-G-Y-P-T.

And He sent a bunch of frogs to E-G-Y-P-T
With a croak, croak here . . .

And He sent some nasty gnats to E-G-Y-P-T
With a scratch, scratch here . . .

And He sent a swarm of flies to E-G-Y-P-T
With a buzz, buzz here . . .

And He made the livestock ill in E-G-Y-P-T
With a sickness here . . .

And He sent some painful boils to E-G-Y-P-T
With an owee here . . .

And He sent some heavy hail to E-G-Y-P-T
With a clunk, clunk here . . .

And He sent some hungry bugs to E-G-Y-P-T
With a munch, munch here . . .

And He sent a darkened sky to E-G-Y-P-T
With a dark cloud here . . .

Moses Had to Let the Pharaoh Know
Tune: "Joshua Fought the Battle of Jericho"

Moses had to let the Pharaoh know,
Pharaoh know, Pharaoh know.
Moses had to let the Pharaoh know
To let God's people go.

Pharaoh Fun

To play this game, you will need two sets of the Moses memory match cards on page 60, a marker for each player, a coin, and the gameboard below. Two or three people may play. Shuffle the cards, and place them facedown beside the gameboard. Each player places his marker on START. The first player turns the top card over, explains the picture to the other players, then flips a coin. She may move one space for heads and two spaces for tails. Then the next player takes his turn. If a player lands on the space at the top of Pharaoh's headpiece, he gets an extra turn. The first player to reach FINISH is the winner.

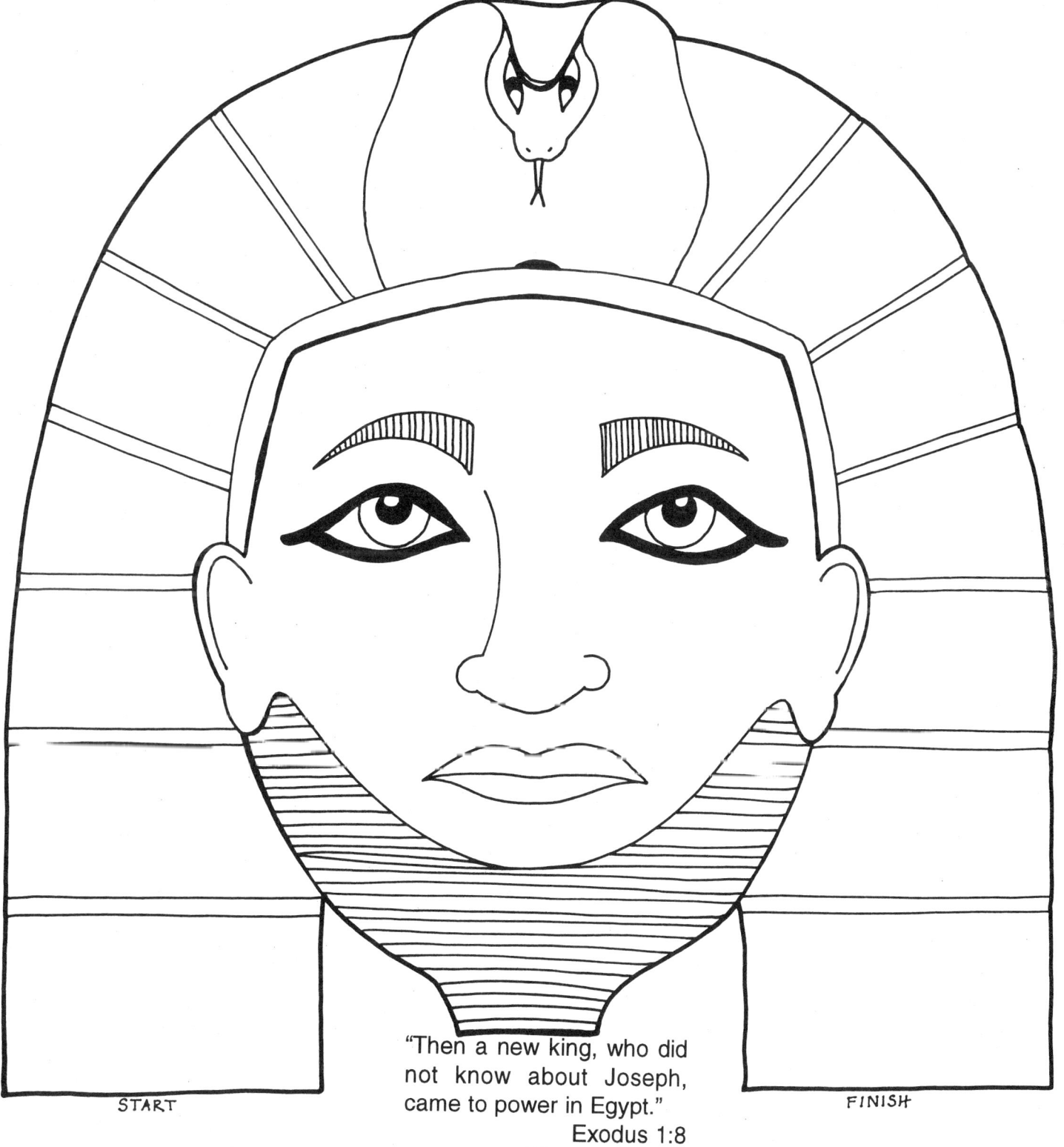

START

FINISH

"Then a new king, who did not know about Joseph, came to power in Egypt."
Exodus 1:8

Moses Memory Match

Make two copies of this page for each pair of players. Back the pages with lightweight cardboard before cutting out the cards. Mix up the cards and place them facedown in four rows. Players take turns turning over two cards. If the cards match, the player keeps the cards. If they do not match, the player turns them facedown again. The winner is the player with the most matched sets.

Moses Masterpieces

Decorate a room or table with these projects, and invite others to your "Bible Hero Museum."

Moses Mural
Divide children into groups, and assign each group a different Moses scene to draw on a section of the chalkboard or on a long roll of paper. Scenes may include Moses in a basket, Moses and the burning bush, Moses and Pharaoh, the ten plagues, and crossing the Red Sea.

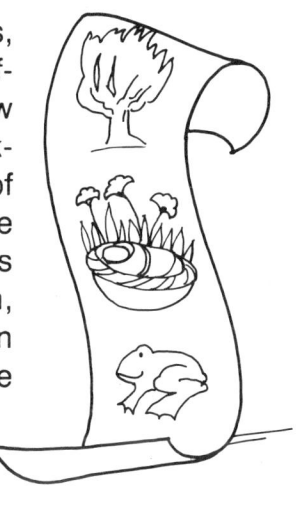

Baby in a Basket
Use paper strips to decorate a small box so that it resembles a basket. Draw the face of baby Moses on a paper circle and place it in one end of the basket. A tissue or paper towel may be placed in the basket to serve as a blanket for baby Moses.

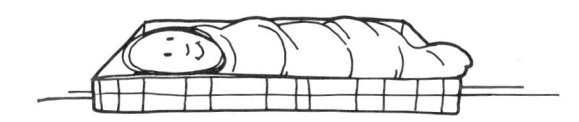

Aaron's Slithering Snake
After telling about Aaron's staff becoming a snake, give children several colors of clay or craft dough. Let them mold pieces of clay into long snakes, using clay of many different colors to add spots, stripes, or other details.

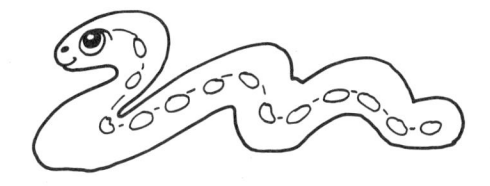

Paper Plate Plague
Fold a paper plate in half. Draw two eyes along the fold as shown. Open the paper plate and cut the eyes along the areas shown with dotted lines in the diagram. Bend the eyes upward. Color or paint both sides of the paper plate green. (Do not color the eyes.) Fold the paper again along the same line. Add a red paper tongue to the mouth. Put your fingers in the holes below the eyes to make the frog's mouth open and close.

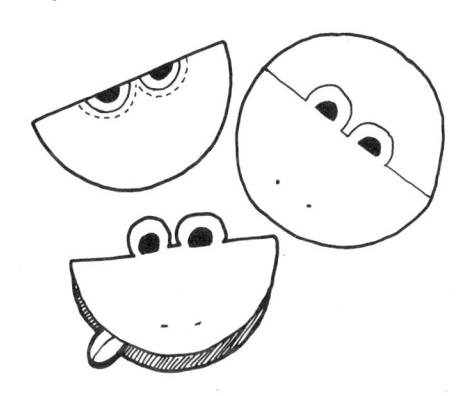

Hailstone Art
Talk about the hailstones and other plagues God sent upon Egypt. Let children use paper punches to make small "hailstones" out of scraps of brightly colored paper. Give the children black sheets of construction paper and some paper-punch "hailstones." Have them glue the "hailstone" dots to the papers to make pictures related to the Bible story of Moses.

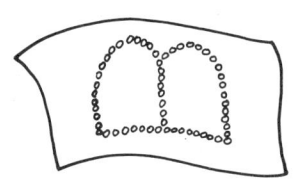

*(These ideas were previously published in *Shining Star* magazine.)

Answers

God Calls Abraham, page 10
"Leave your country, your people, and your father's household and go to the land I will show you."

Abram and Lot's Riches, page 11

The Stars in the Sky, page 12
"Look up at the heavens and count the stars if you can count them... so shall your offspring be."

The Visit, page 13

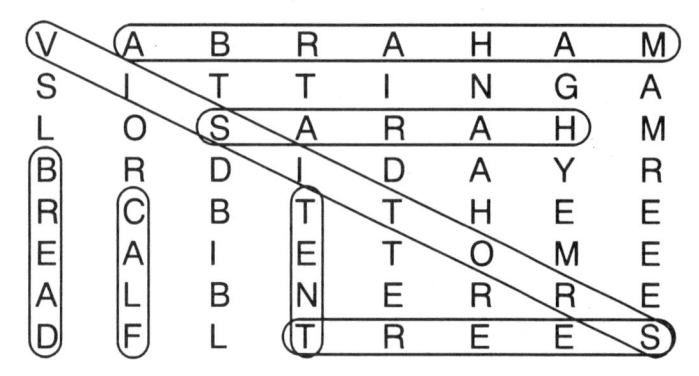

V	A	B	R	A	H	A	M
S	I	T	T	I	N	G	A
L	O	S	A	R	A	H	M
B	R	D	I	D	A	Y	R
R	C	B	T	H	E	E	E
E	A	I	E	E	O	M	E
A	L	B	N	R	R	R	E
D	F	L	T	R	E	E	S

A Name for Abraham's Son, page 14
I S A A C

Rebekah at the Well, page 15

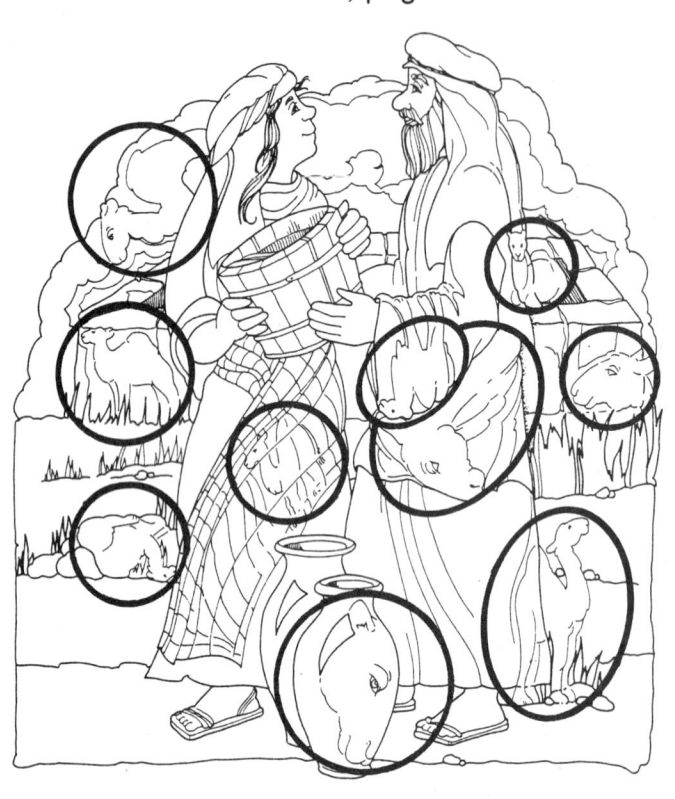

Joseph's Robe, page 29

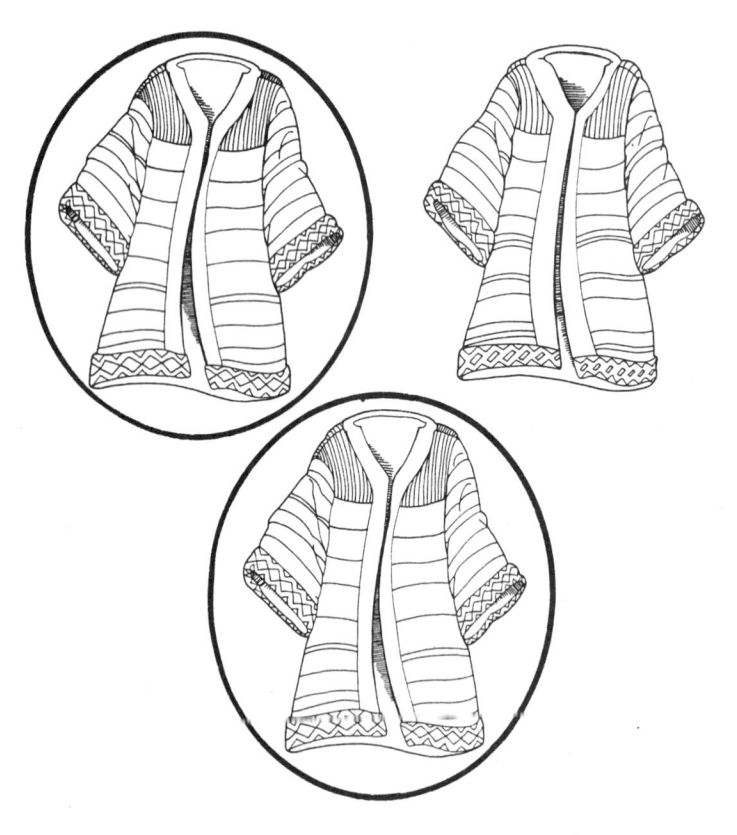

Shining Star Publications, Copyright © 1994   SS3840

Answers

Pulled from a Well, page 30

Hidden Silver, page 33

The Cupbearer and the Baker, page 31

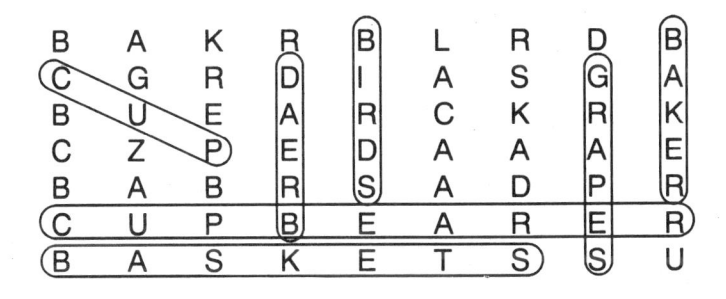

Joseph and His Brothers, page 34

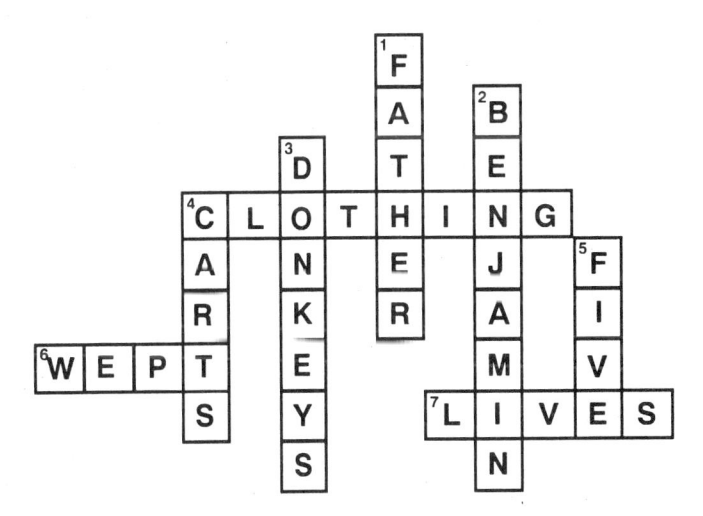

Interpreting Pharaoh's Dream, page 32
"Seven years of great abundance are coming throughout the land of Egypt, but seven years of famine will follow them."

Answers

Slaves, Slaves, page 48

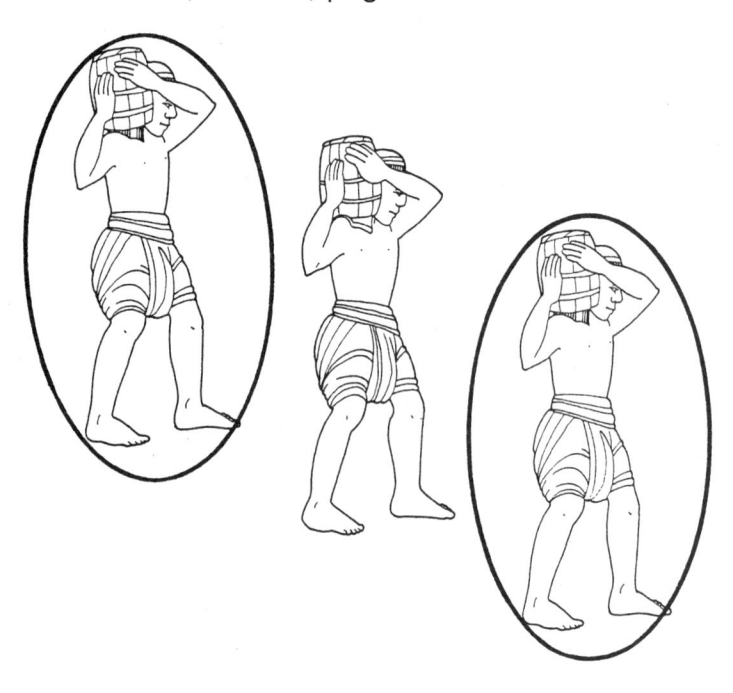

God Calls Moses, page 51

Baby in a Basket, page 49

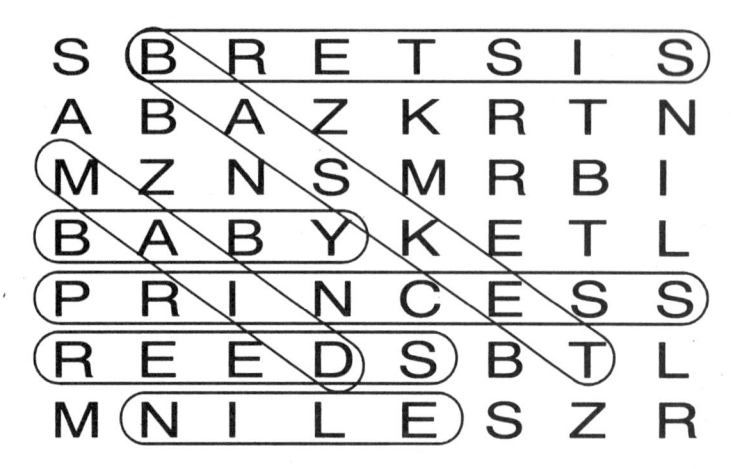

```
S B R E T S I S
A B A Z K R T N
M Z N S M R B I
B A B Y K E T L
P R I N C E S S
R E E D S B T L
M N I L E S Z R
```

Frolicking Frogs, page 52

Drawn from the Water, page 50

Crossing the Sea Crossword, page 53

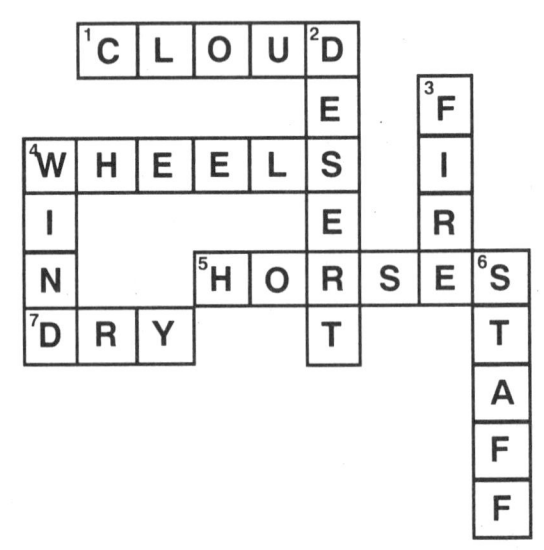

Across: 1. CLOUD, 4. WHEELS, 5. HORSES, 7. DRY
Down: 2. DESERT, 3. FIRE, 6. STAFF

Shining Star Publications, Copyright © 1994   64   SS3840